# PRAISE FOR *COME AND BE FILLED*

With *Come and Be Filled*, Kristopher Whitby has taken a unique and compelling approach to the grand narrative of salvation history. The theme is so common: meals, an everyday event. At the same time, the theme is so profound: how communal eating and drinking are woven throughout Scripture, highlighting important aspects about God and His covenant people. Carefully crafted with well-chosen illustrations and insightful biblical analysis, *Come and Be Fille*d is a deeply satisfying read. Bon appétit!

*Christopher Kennedy, senior pastor, Shepherd of the Hills Lutheran Church, School, and Child Care; author of* Equipped *and* Unfailing

---

Rev. Kristopher Whitby draws on meals, tables, and food to bring us some rich teaching (Law and Gospel) from the inspired stories of Scripture. He writes as a caring and thoughtful pastor with an engaging style, relevant illustrations, and his own personal wit. As I was reading the book, Psalm 34:8 kept coming to mind: "Taste and see that the Lord is good!" Again and again, Whitby takes us to the goodness of the Lord in food, tables, and meals, always enlightening the promises of God in Christ, even when we make a mess. The Lord is good, and this book is good. You'll be glad you read it!

*Rev. Dr. Allan R. Buss, president, LCMS Northern Illinois District*

---

The chapters of this book will open your eyes—and heart—to what it means when you pray, "Come, Lord Jesus, be our guest . . ." As you read and consider how meals shared in Scripture affected the participants, you will also be invited to consider how they affect you. Come and be filled with the bounty of our Lord's grace, told in an engaging and relatable way. Thank you, Rev. Whitby, for this invitation to linger at the table. And don't skip dessert!

*Eden Keefe, president, Lutheran Women's Missionary League*

---

*Come and Be Filled* is a profound exploration of the spiritual significance of shared meals. This book beautifully illustrates how Jesus' presence transforms ordinary gatherings into moments of grace and connection. Through biblical accounts and personal reflections, Rev. Whitby invites readers to experience the joy and depth of dining with Jesus, making every meal a sacred celebration. A must-read for anyone seeking to deepen their faith and relationships around the table.

*Rev. Dr. B. Keith Haney, assistant to the president for Mission, Stewardship, and Human Care, LCMS Iowa District West*

---

# COME AND BE FILLED

## Feasting with Jesus in His Word

KRISTOPHER R. WHITBY

CONCORDIA PUBLISHING HOUSE · SAINT LOUIS

Published by Concordia Publishing House
3558 S. Jefferson Ave., St. Louis, MO 63118-3968
1-800-325-3040 • cph.org

Text © 2025 Kristopher R. Whitby

All rights reserved. No part of this publication may be reproduced, stored in a retrieval system, or transmitted, in any form or by any means, electronic, mechanical, photocopying, recording, or otherwise, without the prior written permission of Concordia Publishing House.

Scripture quotations are from the ESV® Bible (The Holy Bible, English Standard Version®), copyright © 2001 by Crossway, a publishing ministry of Good News Publishers. Used by permission. All rights reserved.

The quotation from the Small Catechism is taken from Luther's Small Catechism © 1986 Concordia Publishing House. All rights reserved.

The quotation from Arthur A. Just Jr., *Luke 9:51–24:53*, Concordia Commentary, is © 1997 Concordia Publishing House. All rights reserved.

Manufactured in the United States of America

---

1 2 3 4 5 6 7 8 9 10 34 33 32 31 30 29 28 27 26 25

*To Marguerita,*
*for the joy and love*
*at our table*

# CONTENTS

# INTRODUCTION

**IT WAS A COLD JANUARY** day off during my pastoral internship in upstate New York. I was in one of the local malls doing some shopping, but I was mainly just passing the time. At lunchtime, I made my way to the food court, grabbed a fast-food meal, and sat down at one of the tables. I had removed my coat and hat and had bowed my head to give thanks to God for the meal I was about to eat when I had the sense that I was being watched.

I looked up from my serving tray and locked eyes with an elderly woman sitting one table across from me. When our eyes met, she said in a thick New York accent, "That was a very nice thing, young man!"

I smiled and was about to say something to the extent that I always seek to give thanks to God for every meal, assuming she was complimenting the fact that I had paused to say grace.

Before I could say one word, she continued, "You took off your hat before eating. You don't often see manners like that in young people today!"

I smiled again, changed my course of thought, shared with her that my parents tried to raise me with some manners, and dove in to whatever food was in front of me.

I thought it funny that the woman had completely missed that I had prayed—or at least didn't mention it. Reflecting back, I wish I would have taken the opportunity to tell her that, for me, the more significant thing was that I was thanking Jesus for the meal before me and inviting Him to "be my guest" at the table.

Perhaps I was seeing that lunch the way we so often see meals today—as just a way to get nourishment into our bodies so that we can move on to the next thing in our day. And let's face it, in our busy lives, that is what meals can become. We grab a doughnut or a piece of fruit (if we're mindful) on the way out the door in the morning, and that's breakfast. We push through lunch to get a project done, maybe scarfing down a sandwich at our desk or in the car. Dinner is a hastily consumed event, rarely with the entire family together, so that we can get the kids off to different places for their practices or rehearsals. In our culture today, meals are frequently reduced to their basic task of merely fueling us for what's next.

When we habitually do this, something vital, something God-given, is lost. Meals can offer so much more than the mere consumption of food. As friends and family gather for a meal, we can deepen relationships, celebrate special occasions, discuss important matters, and experience fun and laughter around the table. In short, we can share life itself. For followers of Jesus, yet another dynamic occurs at meals. The common table prayer that many Christians pray before a meal not only invites our Savior to bless the meal to be eaten but also requests that He come among us at the table as the guest of honor. When followers of Jesus are present at a meal, Jesus draws near and takes His place at the table. He comes both to bless the actual food and to bring His Word of witness through us to touch the lives of those around the table with His abiding grace and presence.

Scripture records accounts of many significant meals, and amazing things happened especially when Jesus sat at meals with people during His earthly ministry. I invite you to journey with me through some of these biblical meals. We'll stand at the doorway and peer into some of the turning points in the story of God's plan of salvation that take place over food. We'll take a seat around the table where our Savior dines and witness what He does and says. Our Lord extends the hospitable invitation to us through His Word to come and be filled, both with the daily bread He provides and with the grace He freely gives. May the Holy Spirit guide us in this journey, deepen our understanding of the grace our Savior extends to those who dine with Him, and show us how He continues to set a place for us all to come and be nourished in His love and in community around the table.

When followers of Jesus are present at a meal, Jesus draws near and takes His place at the table.

Bon appétit!

Chapter 1

# FALLING THROUGH EATING

*Then the eyes of both were opened.*

— GENESIS 3:7 —

**A GOOD MEAL CAN HAVE** a powerful influence on a person's decision-making process. In his book *The Course of History: Ten Meals That Changed the World*, Struan Stevenson writes about the importance of a good meal and persuasion:

> **This is why executives regularly combine business meetings with meals, why lobbyists invite politicians to attend receptions, lunches, and dinners, and why major state occasions almost always involve an elaborate banquet. Churchill called this "dining diplomacy," and sociologists have confirmed that this principle is a potent motivator across all human cultures.**[1]

---

1 Struan Stevenson, *The Course of History: Ten Meals That Changed the World* (Arcade Publishing, 2017, 2019), ix.

Such meals can actually influence world history and, on one occasion, did so to disastrous results.

It happened at a hotel just outside Sarajevo on June 27, 1914. Archduke Franz Ferdinand, heir to the Austro-Hungarian Empire, and his wife, Sophie, Duchess of Hohenberg, were scheduled to visit the city, but reports of a possible assassination attempt moved the archduke to consider forgoing the visit and heading straight home to Vienna. However, that evening, the Ferdinands were served an amazing state meal, which included nine succulent courses and six choice wines, and he decided there at dinner to keep his original plans. Perhaps the sumptuous meal convinced the archduke to continue with the visit to Sarajevo, where he and his wife were indeed assassinated.[2]

This event served as a catalyst for World War I, which resulted in an estimated fourteen million deaths (military and civilian), with another twenty-three million wounded, and exacerbated the spread of the great 1918 influenza pandemic (which may itself have claimed a hundred million lives) through the massive movement of troops around the world. Had one great meal not been eaten by one couple, what disasters might have been avoided! Yet the consequences of this meal pale in comparison to our focus in this chapter. The simplest of meals for one couple brought disaster for all of humanity for all time.

The simplest of meals for one couple brought disaster for all of humanity for all time.

God had made humanity in His image and endowed Adam and Eve with His righteousness, giving them life and the ability to further make life that would also reflect His image. He had

2 See Stevenson, *The Course of History*, 115.

provided His creatures with the means to sustain their lives, and that sustaining—at least in part—would come through eating. "Behold, I have given you every plant yielding seed that is on the face of all the earth, and every tree with seed in its fruit. You shall have them for food" (Genesis 1:29). In fact, the Lord had given Adam a role in cultivating the means through which He would graciously sustain their lives. Yet, with all the plants and trees God had given for food, He had also set a boundary for His creatures, who perfectly bore His image. "The LORD God commanded the man, saying, 'You may surely eat of every tree of the garden, but of the tree of the knowledge of good and evil you shall not eat, for in the day that you eat of it you shall surely die' " (2:16–17). The way they participated in the sustaining of their lives was also the way by which their lives could be taken from them: by eating.

## Enter Satan

And so we come to Genesis 3—the encounter between Satan and Eve. Everything that follows happens as a result of the simplest of meals, eating one piece of fruit.

Moses, the author of Genesis, describes the serpent as "more crafty than any other beast of the field that the LORD God had made" (Genesis 3:1a). In other words, what Satan is about to say is deceptive. Jesus will later call Satan "the father of lies" (John 8:44), and here we see the first record of his lying. It would be easy to conclude that Satan's goal is to wreak havoc on humanity and bring us all down to the eternal condemnation that awaits him. However, his purpose is even more sinister. Satan desires to rob God of the joy of

His communion with the crown of His creation, the love of His life, His created children who bear His image, humans. Satan's strategy? Create separation.

So the serpent opens his mouth and asks Eve, "Did God actually say, 'You shall not eat of any tree in the garden'?" (Genesis 3:1b). Notice what Satan is doing. He's opening a dialogue with Eve based on a false premise. It's an obvious lie; God had said they could eat from any tree in the Garden of Eden except for the one in the middle of the garden. On the day they ate from that tree, they would die (2:17). Yet in asking this question (which should've easily been dismissed by sinless Eve), Satan presents to Eve the possibility that, whatever God had said, it could be questioned, perhaps even changed. Making humans question the Word of God is Satan's key strategy in his attempt to rob God of the crown of His creation.

Making humans question the Word of God is Satan's key strategy in his attempt to rob God of the crown of His creation.

By stepping away from God's Word, Adam and Eve step away from God. But it's more than the fact that God created by His Word in the beginning. As we read in the Gospel of John,

> **In the beginning was the Word, and the Word was with God, and the Word was God. He was in the beginning with God. All things were made through Him, and without Him was not any thing made that was made. In Him was life, and the life was the light of men. . . . And the Word became flesh and dwelt among us, and**

> **we have seen His glory, glory as of the only Son from the Father, full of grace and truth.** (1:1–4, 14)

The Word that Satan invites Eve to question and step away from is none other than the preincarnate Second Person of the Trinity, Jesus. How will Eve respond?

She replies, "We may eat of the fruit of the trees in the garden, but God said, 'You shall not eat of the fruit of the tree that is in the midst of the garden, neither shall you touch it, lest you die' " (Genesis 3:2–3). If only Eve had stopped with her statement about not eating the fruit! But she adds something of her own to the instructions of God: "Neither shall you touch it, lest you die." God had never said Adam and Eve could not touch the tree. It may seem like only a slight change. Perhaps Eve is even expressing a fear of the tree, knowing it somehow relates to death. But Satan does not need Eve to completely abandon God's Word. He's looking for a seemingly small step away. Just enough to make perfection into imperfection. Just enough to make life into death. Adding something to the Word of God would be like taking the incarnate body of the Word made flesh, Jesus, and deciding He needed a third arm or an extra set of ears. It departs from God's design and leads to evil. God Himself warns people not to add or subtract from His Word both in Deuteronomy and Revelation, but of course, Eve doesn't have the benefit of God's written Word. Departing from God's Word always leads to sin, separation, and death, just as it does here.

I imagine Satan's cool coils gently wrapping around Eve's arm, drawing her closer as he feeds her a twisted half-truth: "You will not surely die. For God knows that when you eat of it your eyes will be opened, and you will be like God, knowing good and evil" (vv. 4–5).

Wouldn't it be great to be like God? Let that one sink in. In the past thirty days or so, have you ever once woken up with an ache or pain? Wouldn't it be great to say to yourself, "I think I want to be without pain today," and *bam*! You're completely healed. Or say you woke up one morning and the weather wasn't to your liking. Wouldn't it be great to simply make it a pleasant day? Maybe you don't like the view out your window, so in an instant, you're standing on the beaches of Fiji instead. And even if the weather is a mess in Fiji that day, you're able to make it all to your liking. Wouldn't that be great? I think when most of us sinners think about being "like God," we think of having the all-powerful, all-knowing, all-present characteristics of God at our disposal for ourselves, as if that's what God is like. And in some ways, that is what Satan seems to be offering. He dismisses the truth that God has stated—that on the day they eat of the fruit they will die—even going so far as to state the opposite, that they will not surely die, and insinuate that God is the liar. Then, Satan makes an offer that is only half true at best.

He says Adam's and Eve's eyes will be opened and they will be like God in the sense of knowing good and evil. What he doesn't say is that they will no longer be like God from the perspective of perfectly reflecting His image in their lives. Adam and Eve are already like God in every way possible. God had created them in His image. They are righteous, holy, capable of doing God-pleasing things. He had given them vocations that reflected their likeness to Him by making them stewards of the rest of creation, and He had united them as one flesh in marriage, perhaps as a lesser reflection of His image as the Trinity. God had endowed the crown of His creation with the vocation of making further human life, which would also bear His image. God's perfect design was that humans were to live like this eternally. Before this conversation with Satan, Adam and Eve had been like God! Now they will be like Him in the one way God had not given them: knowing good and evil.

Before this conversation with Satan, Adam and Eve had been like God! Now they will be like Him in the one way God had not given them.

Moses then tells us that Eve, having moved away from God's Word and seeking to participate in Satan's temptation, "saw that the tree was good for food, and that it was a delight to the eyes, and that the tree was to be desired to make one wise" (Genesis 3:6a). How does Eve draw all those conclusions? Whatever her internal thought processes, Eve sets herself in the position to judge what is good, a position that belongs to God, as He revealed about Himself by creating life and judging that it is good. She determines that following Satan's crafty directives will bring her wisdom because she will attain something greater than the life her Creator had given her.

So we come to this simplest of meals.

## A Dinner of Death

"She took of its fruit and ate, and she also gave some to her husband who was with her, and he ate" (Genesis 3:6b). As God's creatures sink their teeth into the fruit of the tree of the knowledge of good and evil, as they literally swallow the lies that Satan has told and ingest what God had commanded them not to, what do they discover? Do they discover that they now command all power and knowledge and that they had pulled themselves to a higher, wiser place than God had given them? Do they find themselves on a level plain with their Creator, addressing Him as His equals? By following Satan and departing from God's Word, are they more like God than they had been moments before? Hardly! "Then the eyes of both were opened, and they knew that they were naked. And they sewed fig leaves together and made themselves loincloths" (v. 7).

Let's digest these verses a little more. As Eve eats of the fruit, she gives some to Adam, who was with her. Adam was not on the other side of the garden, innocently caring for some animals or tilling the soil. He was right there, watching silently as the bone of his bone and flesh of his flesh did what God had commanded them not to do, and he does nothing to stop it. In fact, he participates in it. If Eve's is the sin of commission, Adam's is the sin of omission in that he fails to do the good that would've stopped sin from entering God's creation by simply telling Eve to get away from Satan. Both Adam and Eve bear the responsibility for sin entering the world.

With the reference to their eyes being opened and their knowledge that they were naked, some are drawn to conclude that this original sin is of a sexual nature. However, that's not what's being communicated in verse 7. Adam and Eve are married at the time of their first sin. Even in a fallen world, it's not sinful for husband and wife to see each other without clothing, so while the fall into sin affects humanity's sexuality, Adam and Eve's first sin isn't about sex. The reference to knowing that they're naked connects back to how Moses describes them in their perfect state at the end of Genesis 2. As God joins Adam and Eve in marriage, Moses ends the chapter on a cliff-hanger: "And the man and his wife were both naked and were not ashamed" (v. 25). There is no sin in their lives, so there is no sense of distrust of the other, nor is there a need to feel a sense of shame in who they are, as they perfectly reflect God's image.

Now, having eaten the forbidden fruit, they have not only sinned but also become sinful. In my years of ministry as a pastor, I've often tried to describe what that first awareness of their own nakedness might have been like for our first parents. Perhaps it was like your first time being in a state of undress before someone you didn't know very well, like when a new doctor examines you. Or perhaps it was like that first vulnerable locker-room experience in school. Adam and Eve are ashamed of what their actions have brought them. In an instant, with one small meal, they no longer perfectly bear the image of God. They realize they're different now, and neither feels quite as intimately comfortable with the other. As their shame sets in, they try to cover it (and perhaps their sin) with their own efforts by sewing fig leaves together to create their first clothing items.

In an instant, with one small meal, they no longer perfectly bear the image of God.

The first sin, then, has to do with Satan's goal of separation, and we see that separation bear its tragic fruit in their lives in the next verses.

## Sinners Before the Sinless Lord

**And they heard the sound of the LORD God walking in the garden in the cool of the day, and the man and his wife hid themselves from the presence of the LORD God among the trees of the garden. But the LORD God called to the man and said to him, "Where are you?"**
(GENESIS 3:8–9)

When I was growing up, these were the scariest words that could be uttered in my family: "Wait till your father gets home." When I'd hear my dad's steel-toed boots hit the front porch after being told that, I wanted to disappear rather than face my father's disappointment and anger and the consequences that were sure to come.

The verses above describe a similar but far more heartbreaking experience. Adam and Eve may not fully realize what they've done, but they know things have gone tragically wrong because they ate the fruit. As they hear their Creator drawing near, they know He will be displeased. They seek to avoid God and the consequences they fear will come. The heartbreak comes full circle when we consider God's perspective. God has drawn near to commune with the crown of His creation, and they do not rush to receive Him and His love. They are missing. It's not simply that God is missing out on the joy of His creation, but they are missing from being with Him, which bodes far worse for them than for God. He now asks Adam that telling question: "Where are you?"

God knows where Adam and Eve are. He's not engaging in some divine game of hide-and-seek. He's alerting them to their new reality: "You're not with Me." They have physically separated themselves from God. And as God is their only source of life, if Adam and Eve are not with Him, they will die that day. In fact, they've died in several ways. They've died to the perfect image of God they once reflected. They've died to the life that would've been theirs without sin. They've died to the perfect life they would've given to their children, who will now inherit a sinful nature. They are now in the process (for the first time in all creation) of physically dying, which will one day happen in total, and they are spiritually dead in God's eyes. God had clearly warned them, "In the day that you eat of it you shall surely die" (2:17), because their sin would separate them from Him. Now that they are not *with Him*, they have been cut off from their only source of life, and they die.

Now that they are not with Him, they have been cut off from their only source of life, and they die.

The consumption of food in the garden, meant to sustain life and bond humans together in community and in reliance on their gracious God, has now become the means of separating Adam and Eve from God and shattering their relationship with each other and all creation. We see this in their responses to God's further questioning. When God asks Adam who told him he was naked and whether he has eaten from the forbidden tree, Adam responds, "The woman whom You gave to be with me, she gave me fruit of the tree, and I ate" (3:12). Adam no longer sees Eve as "bone of my bones and flesh of my flesh" (2:23) but rather refers to her more objectively as "the woman." Here, he tries to shift blame not only to his wife but even to God, since God was the one who gave the woman to him. Again, Adam shows he is separated from his wife and from God. Eve's response when God questions her also illustrates how sin has alienated humanity from the rest of creation: "The serpent deceived me, and I ate" (3:13). Both Adam and Eve take no responsibility for their sin and push the blame to others. God's creation has come unraveled, all because of a simple meal.

## Promise amid Pain

God does not ask the serpent any questions. He simply pronounces the terrible results of this sinful meal. As He does so, the Lord weaves a picture and promise of salvation, and images of meals and food are a part of it.

The serpent is to eat dust all the days of his life. To some, this may sound like Moses has written in ignorance rather than by inspiration of the Holy Spirit. Anyone who's taken a basic biology or zoology course can readily point out that snakes do not have dust in their food chain. However, when we recall that the serpent here is Satan and when we consider the rest of the curses for sin, this pronouncement reflects a depth of insight. The curses for sin God announces in Genesis 3:14–19 are bookended with the image of dust. The Lord formed Adam from the dust of the ground when He created him in His image. Now Adam is to return to the ground in death: "For you are dust, and to dust you shall return" (v. 19). Satan's appetite and diet will consist of the death of humanity. Therefore, the serpent will eat dust all his days. Yes, through one meal,

Satan has brought all humanity into the dust of death. God makes such dust Satan's diet, but it's a meal that will never satisfy. And it's a hollow, short-lived victory because, in the midst of these curses, the Lord also announces that, through Eve, He will send the One who will destroy Satan's power over humanity: "I will put enmity between you and the woman, and between your offspring and her offspring; He shall bruise your head, and you shall bruise His heel" (v. 15). Sin and death may have come through Eve taking the first bite of the forbidden fruit, but forgiveness and life will also come through her as her descendant, Mary, will give birth to Jesus, the Savior from sin, death, and Satan!

Through Eve, He will send the One who will destroy Satan's power over humanity.

Adam's part of the curse also relates to food. God had intended that his work of tending the garden and growing food for himself and his offspring would be easy, but now that work would be hard. By the sweat of his face, he was to eat his bread. The ground itself, which was meant to bring forth only that which sustained life for Adam and his community, would be cursed because of his sin. Now the earth would also bring forth thorns and thistles, choking out the life of other plants that would have nourished the community and serving as a painful reminder that Adam's days, too, were numbered.

The Lord paints a graphic picture of what has come of His people eating a piece of fruit and thus disobeying His command—dust, death, and thorns. Yet the image of thorns also plays an integral part in His plan of salvation. In Genesis 22, the Lord calls on Abraham to take his son Isaac—his only son, whom he loves (v. 2)—and sacrifice him on a mountain.

As Abraham raises the knife to carry out the sacrifice, the Lord intervenes and presents Abraham a substitute sacrifice: a ram caught by its horns in thorns. It foreshadows the time when the Lord Himself will take His Son, His only Son, the one He loves, Jesus, and sacrifice Him on the hill of Golgotha. And when Jesus, the Lamb of God, is sacrificed, His head will be crowned with thorns—the curse brought on by Adam's sin.

There's always a nagging question that hangs in the atmosphere surrounding this first and most tragic of meals in human history. Why did God place the tree of the knowledge of good and evil in the garden in the first place? If there's no tree, no command not to eat from it, no resulting sin and death, then humanity lives out history as God intended for His creation, right? Some have suggested that the Lord placing the tree in the garden was a matter of giving free will to humanity. The reasoning goes that if God's perfect creatures were to truly love Him of their own volition, then they had to have the opportunity to not love Him by disobeying His will, even if that disobedience brought death. Hence, the Lord places the tree with the forbidden fruit.

While there may be something to this in the realm of logic, I believe the Lord placed the tree, with its forbidden fruit and His command, not to reveal humanity's free will but to reveal the depth of His own heart for the crown of His creation. It is one thing for God to love creatures who are sinless, righteous, and able to perfectly reflect His own image. It's quite another level of love when the Lord loves creatures

> The Lord places a means in the garden for Him to reveal His deepest love for people, for all creation.

who have lost it all to sin. So, the Lord places a means in the garden for Him to reveal His deepest love for people, for all creation, letting humanity fall into sin so that He might reveal Himself as the God who graciously rescues from sin by His own sacrifice, even unto death on a cross.

Satan deceitfully tempted Adam and Eve with the promise that they would be like God. And in our selfish, sinful nature, we might ask, "Well, wouldn't it be great to be like God?" However, our sinful nature gives us a grossly warped view of what God is like. But wouldn't it be great to be like God when we truly see what God is like? So, the Lord reveals what He's truly like, loving creatures who cannot love Him, bringing them from sin and death to salvation and life through the One who perfectly reflects His image by not falling for Satan's temptations and instead serving His heavenly Father, even to the point of death on the cross and the joy of an empty tomb. Wouldn't it be great to be like Him!

## QUESTIONS FOR DESSERT

What meal in human history would you like to have witnessed?

How are you tempted to desire godlike powers? How does clinging to God's Word help us face such temptation? (See 1 Corinthians 10:13; Hebrews 2:18.)

How does Jesus bear God's image perfectly in His earthly ministry? How does that affect us as His followers? (See Philippians 2:5–11; 2 Corinthians 4:3–6; 5:21; Colossians 1:15–20.)

CHAPTER 2

# A MEAL WITH A FUTURE

*You shall keep it as a feast to the LORD; throughout your generations.*

— EXODUS 12:14 —

**FOR SOME OF YOU, IT** might be the scent of garlicky butter melting on bread and the hints of basil blending with tomato sauce as the lasagna bakes. For others, it's the cozy smell of simmering chicken noodle soup, even if that soup came from a Campbell's pop-top can. My wife and I joke that we love people way too much to ever cook for someone, including each other! However, on those occasions when I come through the door on a cool fall evening and catch the aroma of her chili stewing in the kitchen, I'm transported back in time. Suddenly I'm a kid again, walking into the kitchen of my childhood home with its old linoleum floor and the big, round oak table, and I catch a glimpse of Mom at the stove, fussing over that night's chili dinner. It's powerful. Those feelings of being loved and cared for stay with me as my wife ladles another expression of love and care into a bowl and serves dinner.

Meals have an amazing way of connecting us to our past. The recipe for the Thanksgiving stuffing that was handed down from generation to generation and served every year now cannot be changed because to do so could ruin the holiday. Maybe a bite of a particular brand of pizza takes you back to your family's Friday night tradition, even if decades have passed. I'm sure there are studies that account for the physiological and psychological reasons that food draws up vivid memories even with just its aroma, and we could spend the rest of this chapter tracing those well-worn trails, but this chapter explores a question that takes us down a different path: Do meals always work in only one direction? Do they have the power only to bring us back in time as they trigger memories or deeply embedded emotions? Or are there meals that move forward in time from their first celebration to claim and bless a people not yet born? Here, we'll take a look at one such meal and catch a glimpse of its greater fulfillment in another.

Meals have an amazing way of connecting us to our past.

The meal of our focus was some four hundred fifty years in the making. It all started with a joyful invitation from the king of Egypt—Pharaoh, by the traditional title—who allowed his second-in-command, an Israelite named Joseph, to bring his entire extended family down from the land of Canaan to live in Egypt so that they might be well cared for during a severe regional drought. Joseph's father, Israel (originally known as Jacob), along with his sons, their families, and all their servants, moved down to Egypt in the closing chapters of the book of Genesis. Under God's continual blessing, the family prospered there and grew to be a numerous people as the generations passed.

As Israel grew to be a nation, their once gracious relationship with Egypt chilled and became hostile. Moses writes in Exodus 1:8, "There arose a new king over Egypt, who did not know Joseph." In this new Pharaoh's estimation, the strength and size of Israel living in their midst as a free people made them a threat, as the foreigners might ally themselves with one of Egypt's enemies. His solution was to suppress them by enslaving them. Yet, the tougher he made their enslavement, the more the Israelites multiplied. Pharaoh's next step was literally to cull the Israelite population by instructing Hebrew midwives to kill Israelite baby boys. The midwives resisted committing infanticide, saying that the strong Hebrew women had delivered their babies before the midwives could arrive and carry out Pharaoh's evil plan. So Pharaoh instructed his people to drown the Israelite baby boys in the Nile. Living in such harsh slavery and under the constant threat that their sons would be killed, Israel cried out to their God, and Yahweh responded.

## The Lord Sends a Savior

Yahweh sent them a deliverer in Moses. Moses not only represented God and His people before Pharaoh but also was the spokesman between God and His people. He was their mediator, who himself was rescued by God from Pharaoh's reign of death. When Moses was three months old, his mother placed him in the Nile, but she put him there in a floating basket. Moses was found and rescued by a daughter of Pharaoh.

She adopted Moses as her own son. In fact, she even named him Moses because that name sounds like the Hebrew word for "draw out," which is what she had done. She had drawn Moses out of the Nile and rescued him. Now, Yahweh would use Moses to draw out His people from Egypt and rescue them. And like Moses' own rescue, it would be accomplished through water, as God divided the Red Sea to provide a safe path for His people to escape the pursuing Egyptian army.

In the buildup to that rescue, the Israelites witnessed powerful works of God for their salvation. To convince Pharaoh to release the Israelites from slavery, Yahweh used Moses and his brother, Aaron, to bring about ten plagues, which devastated Egypt. From water turning into blood to frogs, flies, hail, and more, all the plagues were sent to compel Pharaoh to release the people of Yahweh. Yet with each plague, Pharaoh refused to free the Israelites, despite his many promises to do so if only Yahweh would end the most recent plague.

The last plague God sent would be the most painful for the Egyptians and would be the catalyst for God's chosen people to begin their journey of rescue and salvation. God sent the plague of death on the firstborn son of everyone and everything in Egypt:

> **At midnight the Lord struck down all the firstborn in the land of Egypt, from the firstborn of Pharaoh who sat on his throne to the firstborn of the captive who was in the dungeon, and all the firstborn of the livestock. . . . And there was a great cry in Egypt.** (Exodus 12:29, 30)

This final plague was disruptive and devastating. Not only did families suffer the grief of losing their firstborn sons, but the very structure of Egyptian society would come unraveled. The firstborn sons would normally receive the lion's share of their family's inheritance. In a patriarchal society, they were to be the heads of their households and the ones who held higher positions of leadership in their communities. In one night, that structure would disappear for an entire nation as Yahweh's destroying angel entered each home to claim the life of the eldest son.

The death of the firstborn sons might seem like justice served, given that Pharaoh had ordered the sons of Israel to be killed. However, something greater is revealed by the fact that the plague extended to the firstborn sons of the livestock as well. Terror would begin to spread as household after household discovered their firstborn sons dead. Families whose sons had not yet died would have rushed to their animal pens to sacrifice the firstborn male of their livestock in the hope that their gods would then protect their sons—only to find that no such sacrifice would be possible. The Egyptian gods could do nothing, because they were not real. The judgment of the God of Israel was inescapable. Death for the firstborn sons had come, but not to every family in the land of Egypt.

Something greater is revealed by the fact that the plague extended to the firstborn sons of the livestock.

Beginning with the fourth plague, flies, Yahweh provided protection for the Israelites from the plagues. So while the Egyptians dealt with flies, dead livestock, and hail, things were different in the region of Goshen, where the Israelites lived. There was not one fly, not one dead animal, and not one hailstone. While the Egyptians experienced three days of haunting darkness, so dark it could be felt, the Israelites did not; Yahweh provided light for His people. When God sent the final plague, death, the Lord made a distinction between the Egyptians and His people. He preserved the lives of the firstborn sons of Israel, which brings us to this chapter's meal.

## The Passover—the Deliverance Meal

The Passover would alter the very perception of time among God's people. The Lord told Moses and Aaron, "This month shall be for you the beginning of months. It shall be the first month of the year for you" (Exodus 12:2). The name of the month was Abib, or "ear month," because new grain was in the ear of the plant. From this point forward, each new year for Israel would begin with the celebration of the Lord rescuing the Israelites from slavery and death, and that celebration would be anchored in the meal Yahweh used as part of their rescue.

On the tenth day of that month, Israelite families were to select at lamb from among their sheep or goats—a perfect year-old male, without any spots or blemishes. On the fourteenth day of the month, all the Israelites were to kill their lambs at twilight, as darkness began to approach. Darkness is a building theme as God sends the plagues. Exodus 10:15 says the swarm of locusts, the eighth plague, was so vast that "the land was darkened." The ninth plague brought three days of utter darkness. This was more than the sun being blotted by overcast skies or even some miraculous three-day solar eclipse. This darkness was so complete that the Egyptians couldn't even move (Exodus 10:23). The final plague came at midnight, in the midst of darkness, and brought the darkness of death. Yet, at twilight, as the day ended and the darkness closed in, God made a way for His people through the sacrifice of a perfect lamb, which literally entered the body of each Israelite as they ate it and was the sign of God's deliverance.

After the lambs were sacrificed, each family was to take some of the blood of the lamb and put it on the doorposts and lintels of the houses where they would eat the meal. The blood would be a sign to the Israelites and to the Lord; when He saw the blood on the doorframe, He would pass over that house and not send the destroying angel into that home to carry out the judgment of the tenth plague. Therefore, the Israelites were rescued from God's judgment of death not because they were Israelites, nor even because they were God's chosen people. Rather, they were rescued because they were in the homes that were covered by the sign of the perfect lamb's blood, the blood of the very lamb they were eating that night.

The lamb was to be roasted whole and eaten with bitter herbs and unleavened bread. The bitter herbs were a reminder of the sufferings and hard life of slavery God's people were now leaving behind. As for the bread, they had no time to let it rise, so it would have to be unleavened. The Lord told them to eat the meal hastily and while dressed for a journey, with belts fastened and sandals on their feet—in other words, this was a meal of hope, a sign that God's deliverance was at hand.

This was a meal of hope, a sign that God's deliverance was at hand.

That very night, devastated by the plague of death, Pharaoh kicked the Israelites out of Egypt. Later, he would have a change of heart, pursue the Israelites to the edge of the Red Sea, and then send his army into the sea after them. Thus, the Israelites would pass through the waters of the Red Sea as another means of God's rescue as He led them to the Promised Land. But on the night the Israelites celebrated the Passover meal, God's people were set free!

The event of the Passover with its foundational meal was also how Yahweh further formed the identity of Israel. In the events of the Passover and the exodus, God adopted the nation of Israel as His son. As He says in Hosea 11:1, "Out of Egypt I called My son." Thus, the heart of the relationship between God and His people was not only as God to worshipers or king to subjects but also as Father to children—not unlike the families gathered around the Passover meal Yahweh had given them.

This meal, which defined the Israelites as Yahweh's redeemed son, was to be celebrated by Israel every year for the rest of time: "This day shall be for you a memorial day, and you shall keep it as a feast to the LORD; throughout your generations, as a statute forever, you shall keep it as a feast" (Exodus 12:14). To this day, Jewish families around the world gather at tables to celebrate the Passover meal. If the traditions are kept well, the oldest son at the table will ask why this night is different from all other nights. The father of the family will then recount God's rescue of them.

> As they remember what took place, the blessings of the Lord's rescue move forward in time to claim each generation.

The story of the exodus is to be told in the first person. In other words, the father will not say, "Long ago, our ancestors were in captivity in Egypt," but rather, "Long ago, *we* were in captivity in Egypt." Had God not acted then, His people might still be in captivity. This meal, then, ties His people to those historic acts of salvation. As they remember what took place, the blessings of the Lord's rescue move forward in time to claim each generation.

## A Greater Deliverance to Come

Even as the annual Passover meal was to remind God's people of His rescue in the past, it also looked forward to a greater rescue that God had promised to His people from the beginning. And He still ties that rescue to a special meal. Detail after detail of the exodus and Passover meal are fulfilled in Jesus Christ; the parallels are unmistakable. As in the exodus from Egypt, God's chosen people—that is, all of humanity whom He created in love—are enslaved. Jesus Himself declared, "Everyone who practices sin is a slave to sin" (John 8:34). The result of sin is death, and not merely physical death but eternal separation from the Lord, who is the only source of life. Again, Jesus makes this clear in John 8:35: "The slave does not remain in the house forever; the son remains forever." What did Yahweh do to rescue His children? He sent His mediator, Jesus. While Moses represented the Lord to His people, Jesus is the fulfillment of Moses' role in that He is the Lord among His people. While Moses was God's mouthpiece, speaking to Pharaoh to entreat him to release Israel, Jesus enacts God's rescue of humanity by breaking the enslaving bonds of sin and death through Himself.

Lamb was the main course in the Passover meal. Early in Jesus' public ministry, He is identified as "the Lamb of God, who takes away the sin of the world!" (John 1:29). In 1 Corinthians 5:7, Paul declares that Jesus is "our Passover lamb." The lambs were to be perfect, without spot or blemish. Jesus, too, is perfect. The author of Hebrews notes that Jesus was tempted as we are "yet without sin" (Hebrews 4:15). In 2 Corinthians 5:21, Paul states that God made Jesus, "who knew no sin," to be sin for us. Peter writes that "you were ransomed from the futile ways inherited from your forefathers, not with perishable things such as silver or gold, but with the precious blood of Christ, like that of a lamb without blemish or spot" (1 Peter 1:18–19).

The Passover lambs were to be sacrificed at twilight. As Jesus is sacrificed on the cross, from noon until 3:00 p.m., there is "darkness over all the land" (Matthew 27:45), echoing the ninth plague of darkness in Egypt. In the sacrifice of the Passover lambs, their bones were not to be broken (Exodus 12:46). Likewise, after Jesus dies, the Roman soldiers confirm His death by piercing His side with a spear rather than breaking His legs, as they do with the two criminals crucified with Him. John writes, "For these things took place that the Scripture might be fulfilled: 'Not one of His bones will be broken' " (John 19:36). God's people were to eat the lamb's flesh and cover their doorframes in the lamb's blood. Jesus' disciples also receive His blood and eat His flesh through two powerful gifts: Baptism and the Lord's Supper.

Looming in the background of the Passover meal is the final plague, the death of the firstborn sons. The fulfillment of this final plague is also found in Jesus. He is God's only-begotten Son, the firstborn of the virgin Mary. Through the death of the firstborn Son, Jesus, God's adopted sons are rescued by His blood. Paul beautifully states how we are marked with the blood of Christ, which effects our rescue from death through Baptism:

Through the death of the firstborn Son, Jesus, God's adopted sons are rescued by His blood.

> **Do you not know that all of us who have been baptized into Christ Jesus were baptized into His death? We were buried therefore with Him by baptism into death, in order that, just as Christ was raised from the dead by the glory of the Father, we too might walk in newness of life.** (Romans 6:3–4)

Through our Baptism into Christ Jesus, we are called God's sons, just as Yahweh called Israel His son through the rescue of the exodus: "For in Christ Jesus you are all sons of God, through faith. For as many of you as were baptized into Christ have put on Christ" (Galatians 3:26–27).

Finally, the Passover meal finds its fulfillment in the meal of Holy Communion. Christ institutes Holy Communion, the Lord's Supper, at a Passover celebration with His disciples. It is the last Passover meal He will eat with them before His death and resurrection. In the context of this Passover, Jesus gives His very body to eat and His blood to drink.

> **Now as they were eating, Jesus took bread, and after blessing it broke it and gave it to the disciples, and said, "Take eat; this is My body." And He took the cup, and when He had given thanks He gave it to them, saying, "Drink of it, all of you, for this is My blood of the covenant, which is poured out for many for the forgiveness of sins."** (Matthew 26:26–28)

On that night, as Jesus' disciples participate in a meal that has come through time to bring the blessing of God's rescue to them, Jesus institutes a new meal that will cross time to bring the blessings of Christ's rescue from sin and death to God's children, gathered at His table. Paul reflects this as he writes to Christians decades after the first celebration of the Lord's Supper:

> **For I received from the Lord what I also delivered to you, that the Lord Jesus on the night when He was betrayed took bread, and when He had given thanks, He broke it, and said, "This is My body, which is for you. Do this in remembrance of Me." In the same way also He took the cup, after supper, saying, "This cup is the new covenant in My blood. Do this, as often as you drink it, in remembrance of Me." For as often as you eat this bread and drink the cup, you proclaim the Lord's death until He comes.** (1 Corinthians 11:23–26)

With each celebration of this Meal, Jesus' followers remember Him. But this remembrance is no passive reflection, like reminiscing on a good meal of the past. Rather, as Jesus' followers around His Table remember Him and what He has done for their salvation through His life, death on the cross, and resurrection, God the Father also remembers. Through this Meal, God brings to its partakers all the blessings this Meal has always given. Because Jesus is present, body and blood, by His words spoken over the bread and wine by His servant, the pastor, the participants in this Meal are brought into the real presence of their Savior. Now, like each generation of disciples since the first time Jesus gave this Meal, they receive forgiveness of sins because the Lamb of God shed His blood for them. Like all the faithful who have ever celebrated this Meal, they freely receive the fulfillment of God's love for His people in the blessings of life and salvation. And like those who came before them, in their very act of eating the Meal, participants in the Lord's Supper make a public witness to the gift of salvation in Jesus' death, for they "proclaim the Lord's death until He comes"! This faithful witness will remain part of the Christian Church's celebration of the Lord's Supper until that day when Jesus will come back to earth in the final fulfillment of His rescue meal!

As Jesus' followers around His Table remember Him and what He has done for their salvation through His life, death on the cross, and resurrection, God the Father also remembers.

Like God's people who were rescued from Egypt on the night of the first Passover meal, Jesus' followers who gather around His Table to eat and drink His body and blood for their salvation are joyfully awaiting the final fulfillment of this Meal. The Lord's Supper is a foretaste of the feast to come;

it points to a day when our Savior will pull a chair up right next to ours and lovingly put food on our plate. We will hear His voice as He rejoices that we're dining with Him and all His redeemed. As we look around that table, we, too, will rejoice in all we see gathered there and glorify Jesus for His love.

Glance around Jesus' Table next time you're at Communion to catch a glimpse of this blessed future. The saints of our Lord gathered at the communion rail or standing in line next to you waiting to receive Jesus are the same saints who will sit with you at Jesus' heavenly feast! As that particular celebration of the Lord's Supper concludes, be reminded that the day is coming when the feast will last eternally. The firstborn Son of God is no longer dead but lives eternally and will set us at His table to do the same.

Glance around Jesus' Table next time you're at Communion to catch a glimpse of this blessed future.

## QUESTIONS FOR DESSERT

Which food or meal sparks memories for you?

How does the collective witness of fellow believers gathered around Christ's Table strengthen your faith in Him?

Which of Christ's saints are you joyfully anticipating dining with in His heavenly feast?

Chapter 3

# A COVENANT CONFIRMED

*They beheld God, and ate and drank.*

— EXODUS 24:11 —

**IT WAS A DREAM COME** true, even though I hadn't actually dreamed of it beforehand. The church where I served as pastor was hosting the songwriter, musician, and author Michael Card. He's won several awards, including the 1983 Dove Awards for Songwriter of the Year and Song of the Year for "El Shaddai." His music had a strong influence on my faith when I was a young Christian and later when I was a seminarian.

Michael Card had served as the guest musician for our morning worship services, and our church would be hosting his concert that evening. As people were leaving after the late service, Michael turned to me and asked if I had plans for lunch. I'm sure I stammered something about my availability or playing his host or something lame. With that, we grabbed his cellist and were off to find food.

I attempted to play it cool as we piled into my car, but internally, I panicked. While not a Hollywood star or athlete,

Michael Card was by far the most famous person I had ever met. And now I was driving him around, trying to hold a conversation while my thoughts raced: *Where am I going to take him? It has to be someplace nice! What will Michael Card think is nice? What restaurants are even open on Sunday afternoon?*

Before I became completely paralyzed, Michael Card offered a down-to-earth, stress-relieving suggestion: "Kris, is there an Arby's nearby?" Indeed there was, and before long, I had the honor of having a simple meal of roast beef and fries with an amazing Christian artist. It wasn't a meal worth remembering for the quality of food (no disrespect intended to the fine people of Arby's). It was a meal to remember because of the guest and the conversations we had, and that was just with Michael Card. Can you imagine a meal where the main guest and host is God Almighty?

Can you imagine a meal where the main guest and host is God Almighty?

Among Christian and Jewish groups in the Middle East, both in ancient times and today, dining with someone is considered an honor. Sharing a meal means sharing the blessing God bestows on that meal. It is considered a way to share life itself. If you're invited to someone's table, you're considered like family for the host. Time and again during Jesus' incarnate ministry, He sat at table, teaching about the kingdom of God and sharing a meal in an atmosphere of acceptance, forgiveness, and peace. This is nothing new for God. Already at the time of Moses, some fourteen hundred years before Jesus' birth, God shared in a meal with the leaders of Israel. In it, He granted a foretaste of a feast to come!

## The Relationship Defined—Yahweh's Commandments

The scant details of the meal between God and the leaders of Israel are recorded in Exodus 24:1–11. The chosen people of Yahweh, the Israelites, had witnessed and experienced some amazing things before this meal as God brought them out of slavery in Egypt.

God now brings them to Mount Sinai, where He Himself comes to the top of the mountain to give His people His Law. It is a tense moment, to say the least. The Lord instructs Moses to consecrate the people for two days and for them to wash their clothes and to be ready for Him on the third day (Exodus 19:10–11). No one, not even animals, is to touch the mountain, and anyone who does is to be put to death. On the third day of these preparations, the Lord comes down in a fire that covers the mountain in smoke. As He arrives, the people witness lightning and thunder and a trumpet blast so loud that it can be heard throughout the camp. Moses tells us that "all the people in the camp trembled" (v. 16). Amidst this scene of awe, the eternal God speaks His Law that has come to be known as the Ten Commandments.

While entire books have been written on the Ten Commandments alone, and rightly so, several things are worth noting here. At the start of the Commandments, the Lord identifies Himself for the Israelites: "I am the Lord [Yahweh] your God, who brought you out of the land of Egypt, out of the house of slavery" (20:2). As God begins to give the Law that will shape the community of His chosen people and guide their individual and corporate lives, He gives them His personal name, *Yahweh*. The God of the Israelites is not some impersonal force or distant god of mythology; He has personhood and will relate to His people on a personal level. He is also *their* God, indicating that Yahweh sees Himself in relationship with them. He also reminds them that He is their Savior-God because His actions brought them out from Egypt, where they had been enslaved. Their God had rescued them, using Moses as His agent of redemption.

The God of the Israelites is not some impersonal force or distant god of mythology; He has personhood and will relate to His people on a personal level.

It makes sense, then, that the first of the Commandments God gives is that Israel should have no other gods. Yahweh is their Savior-God; no other god brings salvation! Likewise, they are not to make carved images or bow down to them as idols. There are to be no images of gods among them, not only so they will not be tempted to trust other powers but also because they themselves are to be the representation, the image, of the one true God. They had been created in His image, and their lives, now ordered and shaped by His Law, are to reflect Him to the world.

They were to use His name (the Second Commandment) but use it related to His grace and love, as they would be marked with His identity. Where His name was invoked, the Lord promised to show up with His love and grace. And where would God show up? In the context of worship on the Sabbath day, where His Word was to be proclaimed (the Third Commandment). In fact, no work was to be done on that day. It was a day of rest when there would be no distractions from hearing God's Word, and with no work, it would be a weekly reminder that God, not merely their own labor, was what sustained their lives.

With the people's relationship to the Lord set in order, the other commandments now mark how the people would deal with one another in community. First, they were to honor their parents (the Fourth Commandment). The home would be the first place where God's people would learn about their loving God and encounter people who reflected His love in caring for one another. Branching out from there, they were to care for their neighbor's life, family, property, and reputation and maintain a heart that was content with what God had given, so as not to create division through jealous coveting. God was preparing His people for how community was to be done as He brought them into the Promised Land.

With the people's relationship to the Lord set in order, the other commandments now mark how the people would deal with one another in community.

## A Meal Invite from the Covenant-Keeping God

The communal relationship that the Lord was forming with the Israelites at Sinai was predicated on the covenant He had long since promised to them at the time of Abraham. About six hundred fifty years before this mountaintop encounter, God had made a covenant with Israel's ancestor Abraham. Like the covenant at Sinai, that covenant was based solely on the Word and actions of God. He gave Abraham a son, Isaac, even though Abraham and his wife, Sarah, couldn't have children, and she was long past childbearing age. That son would be a living symbol of God giving life where there was no life. Abraham would father a nation (in fact, it's the group standing at the foot of Mount Sinai), and that people would be freely given a land by God (which is where they're heading now). The people would find an abundant life in that land where their families could live in safety. But that land foreshadowed the eternal promised land the Lord would freely grant His faithful people in eternity. How would God's promised covenant be fulfilled ultimately? The Lord had promised Abraham that through just one of his offspring, the promised Messiah, all nations would be blessed. In other words, God's faithful people, the children of Abraham, would include more than just biological descendants of the Israelites. What the Lord was doing with them at Sinai would have worldwide implications for all time. Why not celebrate, and how better to do so than with a meal!

What the Lord was doing with them at Sinai would have worldwide implications for all time. Why not celebrate, and how better to do so than with a meal!

The Lord extends the invitation. It's His covenant. It will be His meal. He provides for everything. He tells Moses whom to invite. The guest list includes Moses' brother, Aaron, who serves as Israel's first high priest before God; Aaron's sons, Nadab and Abihu; and the seventy elders of Israel. From context, it seems that Moses' personal assistant and eventual successor, Joshua, is also in attendance. This group represents both the religious and the community leaders of God's people. Moses is still singled out by God as head among this group, as the mediator between God and His people. Moses will be invited to come nearest to God, and he alone will later be invited by God to journey to the top of the mountain and remain with Him, receiving the full code of the Law from the Lord over a period of forty days.

With the Lord's invitation extended, now Moses conducts a rite to confirm the covenant among the Israelites. He first speaks God's Word and all the rules the Lord had given to the people. The Israelites respond that they will do all that the Lord has commanded. Moses then writes all the Words of the Lord down. The written word was not nearly as common anywhere in the world at this time in history as it is today. These words from God were to mark and shape His people for the rest of time. His Word would not change or be subject to the whims of future leaders nor the circumstances of a given moment in history. God's Word would remain sure because it came from Him, and in order that generation after generation could be sure of that Word, God has Moses put it in writing.

Early the next morning, Moses erects a worship space at the foot of the mountain. As the people wake up, they'll see a space that reflects their relationship to the Lord and to one another. There are twelve pillars of stone, representing the twelve tribes of Israel. At their center, Moses builds an altar. The altar symbolizes that the Lord is at the center of His people. Their relationship to Him defines them as a people and is the foundation for their life together as a people. And it is an altar because

It is an altar because at the heart of their relationship with God and one another is a sacrifice.

at the heart of their relationship with God and one another is a sacrifice. This image finds its echo in how Peter later describes the Christian Church: "As you come to Him, a living stone rejected by men but in the sight of God chosen and precious, you yourselves like living stones are being built into a spiritual house, to be a holy priesthood, to offer spiritual sacrifices to God through Jesus Christ" (1 Peter 2:4–5).

Moses then sends a group of young men to sacrifice burnt offerings and peace offerings of oxen to the Lord. The priesthood that was to come from the tribe of Levi had not yet been formed, so these young men stand in that service. The peace offerings and burnt offerings serve two purposes. According to what Moses later wrote in the book of Leviticus, the peace offering would express thanks to God, and the meat that came from this offering was to be eaten in a meal by all in attendance—that is, the entire nation of Israel. This was an expression of fellowship with both God and one another. But this fellowship, or peace, with God could come only by God's grace. The burnt offering was how God communicated His gift of grace. Burnt offerings were the sacrifices made to cover sin. In grace, God would count the life given up by the animal in the burnt offering as a substitute for the life that should've been forfeited by the sinners who violated God's Law. Such sacrifices pointed to their fulfillment by God Himself when He would send the Messiah promised to Abraham, the Lamb of God who takes away the sin of the world, Jesus.

The Lord tells us in Hebrews 9:22 that there is no forgiveness of sins without the shedding of blood. That truth is graphically carried out by Moses among the people. Moses takes the blood from the oxen that have been sacrificed, pours half into basins, and throws the other half against the altar. Then, in the hearing of the people, he reads the book of the covenant he had written from God. Again, the people promise to do all that the Lord has spoken to them through this book (as if they could ever keep such a promise even for one day!). They solemnly promise to be obedient to God's Word. Then Moses takes the remainder of the ox blood from the basins and throws it on the people!

Can you imagine gathering for worship and everyone being doused with animal's blood by the presiding minister in the middle of the service? It might be the last time you'd attend that church, or at the very least, you wouldn't wear your Sunday best to the next service! Yet something vital is communicated in this seemingly gruesome act. As Moses splashes the blood on the people, he announces, "Behold the blood of the covenant that the LORD has made with you in accordance with all these words" (Exodus 24:8). The blood of the covenant communicated two important messages. The first message was one of pure Law, something to the effect of "As this animal's blood was shed today, so may your blood be shed should you ever violate this covenant you've agreed to with the Lord!" The second message was one of pure Gospel. The blood also communicated, "Because our God is merciful and abounding in steadfast love for you, He allows the shedding of the blood of others (the oxen, in this instance) to be a substitute for your blood, granting you forgiving grace for your violation of the covenant." That may be why the blood covered both the

It was a messy covenant ceremony, but God's relationship with sinners could only come through such a sacrifice.

people and the altar by the time the service ended. It was a matter of life and death, a life for a life. It was a messy covenant ceremony, but God's relationship with sinners could only come through such a sacrifice.

## Dining with the Righteous Lord

Now, covered in the sacrifice of the covenant, God's people have been given peace with God. They dine together in the peace offering meal that bonds them to this gift of God's grace they share and to one another in that same grace. As they do, their leaders attend the meal with the Almighty.

Consider these noteworthy things mentioned about this meal with the Lord in Exodus 24:1–11.

Here's how Moses sets the scene: "There was under His feet as it were a pavement of sapphire stone, like the very heaven for clearness" (v. 10). While Bible scholars have provided insights on what Moses describes here, I find it striking to consider what he *doesn't* describe. Moses gives no details about anything above the feet of God. It almost seems as if he would not dare to even lift his eyes above the level of the Almighty's feet—and this was Moses, God's chosen mediator, who is later described as someone whom God would speak with as to a friend. Moses knew that he and the rest of the banquet guests were sinful creatures invited to the table of the holy God. Such moments call for great humility.

Moses then notes that Yahweh "did not lay His hand on the chief men of the people of Israel" (v. 11). Most of us have never attended a special banquet and thought, "Hey wow! The host of the meal didn't kill any of us today!" It's simply not something you'd expect at a dinner. So, why does Moses make note of it as they eat with God? Again, Moses is fully aware that these leaders of Israel are all sinners who are now reclined at the table of the sinless, holy God of the universe. In the presence of the Lord, all sinners might rightly expect the blast of His righteous judgment to destroy them. Yet as the covenant between the Lord and His people is confirmed, He graciously allows the sinful leaders of His sinful people not only to enter His presence but even to eat with Him. In order for this fellowship meal to happen, the Lord must grant these leaders His sanctifying grace, which covers their sin and preserves their lives as they sit in His presence.

In order for this fellowship meal to happen, the Lord must grant these leaders His sanctifying grace.

Finally, Moses says that they actually beheld God and ate and drank. A few chapters later in Exodus 33, God instructs Moses that no one can see the Lord's face and live. And even later, Paul writes in 1 Timothy that God lives in unapproachable light and that no one can see God. Yet here, Moses shares twice that, with eyes averted, the leaders of Israel actually see God as they dine at His table. Moses doesn't note the place settings or the menu. The only focus is the Lord Himself as He provides a meal that connects His people to Himself in grace.

It is a hopeful, well-intentioned promise the Israelites make to the Lord that day at Sinai. They vow under the blood of the covenant to do and obey everything the Lord had said, both the Commandments and the whole legal code given through Moses. Yet not one generation throughout the entire history of Israel, not one single Israelite, would perfectly keep this promise. According to the legal understanding of the day, the fate of the animals sacrificed should have been the fate of those who did not faithfully keep God's covenant. God is not oblivious to His people's sin. Though He can justifiably condemn them before the vow even leaves their lips, our Lord does just the opposite. Before their failed vow is made, the Lord provides a sacrifice—a burnt offering to show that He will cover their sin with the blood of another, foreshadowing His promised Messiah.

When the Messiah comes, He will keep the whole of God's Law perfectly on behalf of all people and be the perfect sacrifice for all people's sin. God's people will be forgiven, and the Holy Lord will suffer His failed, sinful people to dine with Him on the mount. The meal here at Sinai foreshadows that same mercy from God, which permits His failed, sinful, yet forgiven people to dine at His table around the world today and forevermore.

God's people will be forgiven, and the Holy Lord will suffer His failed, sinful people to dine with Him on the mount.

## QUESTIONS FOR DESSERT

Have you ever been at a dinner where the guest of honor was more exciting to you than the meal itself? Did your experience at that meal meet your expectations?

______________________________________________

______________________________________________

______________________________________________

______________________________________________

______________________________________________

Why are we not to fear drawing near to our holy God as we approach His Table at worship? (See 1 John 1:8–2:2.)

______________________________________________

______________________________________________

______________________________________________

______________________________________________

______________________________________________

How might the Lord's grace for you at His Table shape how you receive guests at your own table?

______________________________________________

______________________________________________

______________________________________________

______________________________________________

______________________________________________

## CHAPTER 4

# WHEN FLOUR AND OIL CAN'T SUSTAIN

*But first make me a little cake of it and bring it to me.*

— 1 KINGS 17:13 —

**IF YOU'RE READING THIS BOOK** and you're not a follower of Jesus, wow! Thank you for reading the first three chapters without dismissing it! I hope you'll be richly blessed and come to know Jesus a little better through this work. Chances are, however, that if you're starting chapter 4, you're a Christian. You trust that Jesus is true God and true man, that He lived a sinless life and was crucified, and that His death brings God's forgiveness to all who trust in Him. You also believe that Jesus rose from the dead and will return one day, and when He does, all people will rise from the dead with glorified bodies (like His after His resurrection), and He will take you and all who believe in Him into eternal life!

This is all to say that you have a formed view of the afterlife and your concept of time is linear. You see history as having an end point, of all things coming to some God-ordained fulfillment, and that one day all things on earth will come to their conclusion.

But imagine if that wasn't your view of history or time or even Jesus because you had no thought of Him at all. Imagine if you had no real concept of an afterlife, yet you believed there were gods who possessed powers that could bless you. If life terminated with death and there was no final chapter to history, what would be the greatest blessing some god could provide? A long and happy life filled with prosperity and pleasures—and perhaps maybe a thought to your offspring having the same—would likely best outcome of such a worldview.

Imagine if that wasn't your view of history or time or even Jesus because you have no thought of Him at all.

Welcome to the ninth-century religion known as Baalism.

Baal was the main god of this ancient Semitic religion. His proper name was Hadad or Haddu, which, when translated, probably meant something like "the Thunderer." He was commonly known by his title, Baal, which literally means "lord" or "husband/master." Baal was the god of the storm. His weapons were lightning bolts, and his voice was thunder. He sent the rains, which, from the ancient world's viewpoint, meant he gave life to crops and livestock. This made Baal the god of fertility. I've heard it said that farming, even today, is all about one thing: sex. Plants need to pollinate. Livestock need to breed. In the ancient world, children would have been seen, at least in part, as hands to help with the farm, so the more the better. Baal, the provider of rain, played an important role in making sure all that life happened.

With no concept of an afterlife, Baalism necessarily focused on the here and now of sustaining life and, if possible, having a life that was prosperous. People looked to Baal and other gods to make the land and people fertile in order to produce that prosperity. But how could you get the gods to act on your behalf so that your crops would grow, your livestock would reproduce, and you would have children? Baalism taught that its followers got the gods on their side through devotion, worship, and sacrifices. Since the goal was getting things to produce for your benefit, worship included ritualistic sex with shrine prostitutes, with the idea that the worshipers' acts would inspire the gods to act likewise. And the gods' activity would move the forces of nature so that life would have abundance.

A religion that claims sexual activity will bring wealth and abundance would likely find many adherents in the modern world. And this was exactly the ancient pagan faith being promoted among the people of Israel by their king, Ahab, and his pagan queen, Jezebel (see 1 Kings 16:30–32).

## Exchanging Prosperity for Eternity

It was a radical shift in Israel's worldview and faith. The Israelites had been followers of Yahweh. Whereas the chief concern of Baalism was fertility, the chief concern for followers of Yahweh was having a relationship with Yahweh Himself.

That relationship between Yahweh and His people held two points of tension. First, as a just and holy God, Yahweh does not abide those who violate His laws, but the Israelites, like the rest of humanity, constantly failed to live up to Yahweh's sense of right and wrong. Not only were they constantly sinning (and thus inviting Yahweh's wrath rather than His blessing), but they also were in their very nature sinful, just like the rest of humanity.

This brought the other primary tension into play. Yahweh is eternal, yet because of their sin, His chosen people are temporal. Even a temporally prosperous life would eventually end. The temporal blessings of bumper crops, growing flocks and herds, and large families—all the stuff that Baalism promised in vain—one day will not sustain the person who receives them. Eventually the blessings won't matter anymore because the blessings will be there but the person won't. Death because of sin is the reality for everyone.

How were the tensions of holiness and sin, life and death to be reconciled between Yahweh and His people? Such tensions could be resolved only by Yahweh Himself, and His actions would reveal His very heart for His people.

Such tensions could be resolved only by Yahweh Himself, and His actions would reveal His very heart for His people.

Yahweh is not only a God of justice and holiness who abhors sin and the death it brings. He is also the God of grace, mercy, and love. In fact, these traits are at His very heart. He desires that His relationship with His people—a relationship that also happens to provide them with every blessing they enjoy—would last eternally. So, He will reveal through His Word a promise and plan that He will rehearse for His people time and again throughout their history together and will one day bring to complete fulfillment. It's the plan and promise to send His people a Messiah, a Savior, whose sacrifice in death for the sins of the people will perfectly satisfy Yahweh's just requirement that sin be paid for. This plan also reveals Yahweh's perfect love for His people because Yahweh Himself will be the Messiah and allow Himself to be the sacrifice for their sin. With sin forgiven through Yahweh's blood-bought grace, death no longer means permanent separation. The relationship will last eternally because God's people will now live eternally, like God Himself.

It's a far cry from the here-and-now theology of Baalism. But the fulfillment of Yahweh's plan is still centuries away for the ninth-century Israelites, and the people have fallen in love with the false pagan religion that promises a prosperous life through sexual activity—with their king and queen leading the way. What does Yahweh do? He sends the prophet Elijah.

Elijah, whose name literally means "Yahweh is my God," bursts on the scene like an ancient version of an action hero. Bearing the Word of the King of the universe, Elijah is Yahweh's answer to Ahab and Jezebel's Baalism campaign. Elijah delivers a message to Ahab from Yahweh that is a direct assault on Baalism: You say Baal is god of the storm and therefore the source of fertility and life? Nonsense! At Yahweh's word, there will be no rain in the region, and only by the command of Yahweh will the rain be restored (1 Kings 17:1). No sacrifice, no sensual worship service, no act of devotion from the followers of

> Yahweh is the only real and present God, and He is acting powerfully on behalf of His people to draw them back to a relationship with Him.

Baal will stimulate Baal to do anything about this drought because Baal is powerless. In fact, he doesn't even exist apart from the imagination of his followers. Yahweh is the only real and present God, and He is acting powerfully on behalf of His people to draw them back to a relationship with Him.

Israel and the entire surrounding region move into a drought that lasts for three years. Knowing this will rouse the wrath of Ahab and Jezebel, Yahweh sends Elijah into hiding at the brook of Cherith. There, he has a temporary source of water, and the Lord commands ravens to bring him bread and meat each morning and evening.

At this point you may be thinking, *Finally! The meal that this chapter is all about!* And while it is fascinating that the Lord uses this method to sustain His prophet, the divinely appointed meal that draws us to sit with Elijah is not part of his bird-secured meal plan.

## God's Abundance with Limited Means

Eventually the brook where Elijah is hiding dries up from lack of rain. Yahweh then provides for Elijah through even more unlikely means. The Word of the Lord comes to Elijah again: "Arise, go to Zarephath which belongs to Sidon, and dwell there. Behold, I have commanded a widow there to feed you" (1 Kings 17:9).

Zarephath was a pagan city north of Israel, along the Mediterranean coast. The inhabitants there would have followed Baalism, and they, too, were in the grip of the drought that had come through the prophet's message. While sizable, Zarephath was not an important city to its regional rulers, so it was not likely a high priority for any drought-relief efforts. It's to this unlikely place that the Lord sends His prophet to receive relief from an even more unlikely person.

Widows in the ancient world were rarely in a good situation. In general, women at the time had no rights or means to provide for themselves. They relied on the men in their families to provide for them—usually a father, a husband, or an adult son. Without a husband, widows often had to depend on the kindness of extended family to survive, and that support didn't always come. The widow to whom Elijah is sent seems to be in this predicament and worse. She and her family—one son, and perhaps at least one daughter as well—have no one to care for them in the midst of a devastating drought.

Scripture tells us that somehow Yahweh has already communicated with this widow, commanding her to feed Elijah when he showed up in her town. Can you imagine that encounter? Here is a lady who knows she's run out of the means to sustain herself and her children. As she faces the pain and grief of her circumstances, she receives some strange contact with the God who has caused her dire situation. He tells her she is to use whatever means she has left to provide food for the very man who has been God's instrument in bringing about the drought. It sounds impossible! And that is exactly the point. Yahweh will sustain life where there is no humanly possible way of doing so.

Yahweh will sustain life where there is no humanly possible way of doing so.

As Elijah enters the city gate, he meets the widow as she gathers sticks for firewood. He crosses a few cultural boundaries to initiate a conversation with her. Men were not to speak with women who were strangers, and this prophet of God certainly could have considered himself above talking with this pagan. Despite these barriers, Elijah speaks to her and requests a drink of water. It may seem simple, but the widow herself and even the vessel with which she'd bring the water would be considered unclean for an Israelite to use—yet another boundary crossed to build a connection between Yahweh's prophet and the pagan widow. And in a drought, even the simple request for a drink must have seemed like a burden to the widow. Yet it was also the beginnings of her trust being built in Elijah's God.

Now Elijah pushes beyond the widow's limits of hospitality. As she goes to get him the drink, Elijah also asks for a morsel of bread. You can almost see this poor woman freeze in her footsteps as her mind races to her home and the place where she stores her oil and flour, mentally looking inside both containers and knowing there's not enough to feed her family. How could he ask? How could she obey his God and comply? In her response, she reveals that she is indeed the woman with whom Yahweh had communicated, but she also reveals that this request is overwhelming:

> **As the LORD your God lives, I have nothing baked, only a handful of flour in a jar and a little oil in a jug. And now I am gathering a couple of sticks that I may go in and prepare it for myself and my son, that we may eat it and die.** (1 KINGS 17:12)

Perhaps this widow had thought her encounter with Israel's God a figment of her imagination. Even if she had believed it to be real, maybe she had hoped that she'd be out of the means to feed the prophet and maybe even dead before he arrived. But here he was, standing at the city gate, fulfilling what she had heard from his God. How was she to do what his God had commanded her?

She tells Elijah the truth. There isn't enough to keep any of them alive. In fact, there is only enough for the simplest of last meals for her and her son before they face starvation. Her grief and fear must have been evident because Elijah tells her not to fear. His response offers comfort and a witness of his confident faith in his God. Yahweh was the God who controlled the rain and stopped it. He was the God who had kept His prophet alive by ravens bringing him food. This God would not fail to keep His promises to them.

Elijah then tells her how this will happen. She is first to make a cake of bread for Elijah and bring it to him. Then she is to prepare the meal for her family as she said. Elijah tells her that she can do this because his God has promised that her jar of flour and jug of oil will not run out until the day that the Lord ends the drought.

With little to lose except a final meal, the widow follows Elijah's directions. As she responds in trust, the Lord does not fail her or her family. "And she went and did as Elijah said. And she and he and her household ate for many days. The jar of flour was not spent, neither did the jug of oil become empty, according to the word of the Lord that He spoke by Elijah" (vv. 15–16). Here is this destitute woman with no one to care for her or her children standing

As she responds in trust, the Lord does not fail her or her family.

on the threshold of hopelessness. She uses the last of her flour and oil to bring Elijah a small cake of bread and then makes what must have seemed like a useless trip back to her home to discover that the jar and jug now contain enough to feed her household. I would imagine those first cakes of bread for her family were mixed with a few of the grateful mother's tears as hope returned for this widow.

Elijah's God had made good on His word! Life would continue where there should have only been death. As she takes Elijah into her home as a temporary tenant, she finds Yahweh is faithful, keeping His word time and again, supplying her and her family each day with their daily bread.

## A God Beyond the Temporal

The widow of Zarephath had likely been raised to believe that the gods could provide temporal goods and supplies to sustain life. As she and her family weathered the drought with Elijah in their home, she may have realized that, between Yahweh and Baal, following Yahweh was the better deal. Baal wasn't sending the rain needed to make crops and livestock grow and thus make food for her family available and affordable. Yet right in her own home, Yahweh was providing a supernatural way for her family to eat every day, and He had promised to do so until He sent rains again.

Right in her own home, Yahweh was providing a supernatural way for her family to eat every day.

She might have easily decided to follow Israel's God (or perhaps to follow both gods to hedge her bets) as her temporal provider. But she would have been doing so with the same view of life and history that she had been taught to believe under Baalism. She would have trusted Yahweh to supply for her life and the lives of her family until life ended. Then, it would be all over, and she'd simply cross over into oblivion when she breathed her last.

However, Elijah's God would now reveal the shockingly different truth about life, time, history, and how wonderfully different He is compared to Baal. Each day flour and oil would be found in her kitchen. She and her family could eat to their fill, and with that, I'm sure hope and joy returned to her home. But how long could that last?

Now a crisis hits that no god from her religious background could address: "After this the son of the woman . . . became ill. And his illness was so severe that there was no breath left in him" (1 Kings 17:17).

Despite a seemingly endless supply of food from the hand of God, this widow could not keep her son alive. In her culture, her son would have been the hope of their entire family. If he made it to adulthood, he would be the one to find work, care for his mother in her old age, and help any sisters by arranging marriages so that they, too, would have families to care for them. The minutes would have felt like hours as this woman hovered around her sick son, watching life slowly ebb from his body. The grief no parent wants to face would have mingled with the fear of what lay ahead for her and her family until that unthinkable reality arrived. The breath of her son had left him.

As any parent who holds the lifeless body of their child might, this widow searches for an answer as to why this should happen. In the storm of her pain, she concludes that Yahweh and His prophet must have been the source of this loss and grief. "What have you against me, O man of God?" she asks Elijah. "You have come to me to bring my sin to remembrance and to cause the death of my son!" (v. 18). In the cry of her hopeless pain, she may have been reflecting an incomplete understanding of the God she was coming to know through Elijah.

She had probably heard Elijah speak of God's Law, of how sin entered the world and how sin brings death. She may have been applying her newfound and limited understanding of Israel's God to her terrible circumstances. If only Elijah had not come to her, maybe his God wouldn't have brought her hope in His provision only to dash it with the death of her son once He learned the secret sins of her heart. If Elijah's God had left her alone, she and her son still would have died, but at least they would not have had their hopes and expectations for life raised with the supply of food.

Now, all seems lost, and like many grieving parents, this widow finds a way to simultaneously blame God and herself. In so doing, she touches on the underlying issue. This death, like all deaths, is about sin, and it is seemingly hopeless because there is no way back from death.

This death, like all deaths, is about sin, and it is seemingly hopeless because there is no way back from death.

Struck with his own grief at the boy's death and the woman's suffering, Elijah takes the lifeless boy from his mother's arms and carries him to the upper room, where he had been lodging in their home. He holds nothing back from his God in his anguished prayer: "O Lord my God, have You brought calamity even upon the widow with whom I sojourn, by killing her son?" (v. 20). Elijah takes the widow's cause up as his own and pours out their hopeless situation before the only one who can address it. Elijah then stretches himself out over the lifeless child three times and asks Yahweh for a miracle that had never happened before at that point in history—making a dead person alive again! How does the God who first breathed the breath of life into humanity respond? "The LORD listened to the voice of Elijah. And the life of the child came into him again, and he revived" (v. 22).

When this family had faced starvation, Elijah had the honor of bringing the widow the good news that Yahweh would provide food for her and her family. Now what exceedingly good news he is able to bring her! He brings the boy down from the upper chamber and delivers him to his mother with this wonderful message: "See, your son lives!" As the gaping hole of grief in her heart floods with the joy of life restored, the widow makes a bold confession of faith: "Now I know that you are a man of God, and that the word of the LORD in your mouth is truth" (v. 24).

Life around the table, enjoying the means our Lord provides for life to continue, is a sojourn. It's filled with times of hardship, uncertainty, joy, and hope, but for each person around the table, no matter how loved he or she is by those who fellowship there, the journey eventually ends. At that point, no amount of nourishment from the blessings of that table will be able to sustain that loved one. Death is not simply the end of a temporal life, something that could be avoided with the right temporal

Life around the table, enjoying the means our Lord provides for life to continue, is a sojourn.

means to keep life going. Death is the end of a relationship between the one holy, just God and His fallen, sinful creatures.

Yet death is not the desire nor the delight of God. He would have the joy of the table and of life itself continue beyond the loss of temporal life, and He alone has the power to make that happen. He did so for a grieving widow in Zarephath almost three thousand years ago. In restoring her son from death to life, the Lord not only gives a picture of His desire for all mothers and their children, but He also foreshadows how He will set that eternal table for His own children. One day, the breath would leave the body of His only Son, whom He had sent to save His people. And three days later, that Son would return to life to bring the gift of life everlasting to the world.

In His death and resurrection, Jesus restores the relationship between the one true God and His sinful creatures so that they might fellowship eternally! It's the difference between a circular and linear view of time, between a life that ends with the here and now and life that goes on for all time, and between the false god Baal and the true God, Yahweh, who desires that you be at His table forever.

## QUESTIONS FOR DESSERT

How might Baalism's focus on a prosperous life of pleasure be received in today's world?

When you feel secure in the temporal means to sustain your life, how does that shape you in your relationship with the Lord?

How has the Lord used hardships and sufferings in your life to reveal His faithfulness to you?

Chapter 5

# When Sinners Host a Party for God Incarnate

*For I came not to call the righteous, but sinners.*

— Matthew 9:13 —

**MANY THINGS COMMONLY HAPPEN WHEN** friends get together for a meal. They may laugh, tell stories, revisit memories, add another building block to their relationship, and, of course, nourish their bodies with food. Yet something more happens when Jesus is at a meal. When Jesus—God in the flesh—sits at the table, something far more life-giving than food is present. Jesus comes to the table of sinners and brings the gifts of salvation and sanctification, as we will see when He calls Matthew and encounters a man named Zacchaeus.

In the days of Jesus' incarnate ministry, the Israelites considered tax collectors the scum of the earth, and for good reason. The Roman Empire would collect taxes from the people they had conquered by employing individuals from the conquered people. The Romans would divide up an area and then auction off the right for some citizen of that region to collect Rome's taxes.

The tax collector's job was to guarantee that the Roman overlords received their assessed revenue. As their reward, the tax collectors could charge their fellow citizens extra, which they would keep for themselves, all with the enforcement of Roman military might. So tax collectors were not only considered traitors to their people, but they were also seen as using foreign power to legally rob their neighbors. Being a tax collector for Rome could be financially lucrative, but in first-century Israel, it also meant being a social outcast.

Being a tax collector for Rome could be financially lucrative, but in first-century Israel, it also meant being a social outcast.

Matthew, the guy who would become one of Jesus' twelve apostles and the author one of the four Gospels in the Bible, was a tax collector. From the Gospel according to Luke, we learn that Matthew was also known as Levi, which may indicate that Matthew was from the priestly tribe of the Levites. And judging by Matthew's command of the Hebrew Scriptures as reflected in his own Gospel, it's possible he had some sort of rabbinical training. To the Jewish people who knew him, Matthew would have been like a modern-day minister who began persecuting the church.

And who knew Matthew? Peter and Andrew, James and John would have known Matthew! The Gospel of Mark tells us that Matthew was at his tax collector's booth when Jesus found him and called him as one of His followers. This booth was likely located right along the Sea of Galilee, where Jesus was walking and teaching the crowds. The reason his booth was on the Sea of Galilee? There were two types of tax collectors in Israel: those who collected the property tax and those who collected a tax on goods and services. The bigger money was usually made by those who taxed goods and services. If Matthew's booth was located on the shores of Galilee, he likely would have been taxing the goods coming out of the sea. In other words, Matthew probably would have been collecting taxes from Jesus' disciples, who fished in Galilee.

## From Scumbag to Apostle

You might imagine, then, the surprise it would have been for Matthew to hear Jesus call, "Follow Me" (Matthew 9:9). To be someone's disciple was more than a title. To be a disciple meant more than learning what your rabbi taught; you would also seek to follow his ways, do whatever he did, and put his teachings into practice in your daily life. For Matthew, like the other disciples, it would mean leaving his entire way of life as a tax collector and beginning a new way of living.

Matthew not only leaves his tax collector's booth and follows Jesus, but he even joyfully hosts a great feast in Jesus' honor, and Jesus graciously attends.

Matthew not only leaves his tax collector's booth and follows Jesus, but he even joyfully hosts a great feast in Jesus' honor, and Jesus graciously attends. Whom else does Matthew invite?

Certainly, Jesus' other disciples would be welcomed to come with Him. You can almost imagine their discomfort as these Galilean fishermen gawk about the wealthy home and dine on the feast that was provided through their own hard labor. I imagine Peter eying the fine furnishings in Matthew's home and whispering to John, "Our big catch last fall bought that. . . . Our catch this past spring bought that."

But who else makes Matthew's guest list? He would have been an outcast to any decent part of the community, so he would have invited those who had been willing to associate with him. He invites the outcasts of the community, fellow tax collectors and others who would have been deemed sinners by the upright.

To understand what unfolds next at this dinner party, it's helpful to have a mental picture of many first-century Israeli homes. Many homes were built in the shape of a square or rectangle with an open-air courtyard in the center. Matthew's home was likely constructed in this way. Larger meals would be served in that courtyard, and those passing by could peek through the entry gate and see the party happening.

That appears to have happened in Matthew 9. A group of religious leaders sees the group dining at Matthew's table. The Pharisees and their scribes begin to grumble at Jesus' disciples, "Why does your teacher eat with tax collectors and sinners?" (v. 11). Here is the tension in Jesus coming to Matthew's home to celebrate that he has become one of Jesus' disciples. Due to his profession, Matthew would have been considered unclean by the Pharisees, and now they witness Jesus in the home of that unclean person.

From the Pharisees' perspective, Matthew was stealing from God's people and, worse, giving part of the stolen goods to Israel's conquerors. For the Pharisees, the Romans ruling over God's chosen people brought a festering implication that the Lord was punishing His people for not following His Law well enough. Why else would He have allowed them to be conquered? Thus, by exacting the Roman tax from them, Matthew was unclean as part of a system that oppressed God's people and defied the one true God.

Unclean Matthew was not allowed in their homes or invited to their parties. He was seen as cut off from God's holy people. He would not be welcomed at the local synagogue to hear God's Word. He would certainly not be welcomed to enter the temple in Jerusalem and participate in sacrifices, which were the means God used to offer His people forgiveness. Therefore, Matthew and anyone who associated with him was to be considered cut off from the one true God and all the blessings of being with Him.

Yet Jesus called Matthew, willingly accepted his invitation, entered his home, and ate with Matthew and all the other unclean sinners who were at the meal. From the Pharisees' perspective, Jesus had voluntarily made Himself unclean as well. This meant that He, too, might well be cut off from their God and the blessings of a relationship with Him.

> **From the perspective of Matthew and his party guests, Jesus had granted them an amazing blessing.**

However, from the perspective of Matthew and his party guests, Jesus had granted them an amazing blessing. Someone considered righteous in Jesus' day would never have consented to eating with someone considered a sinner. Each participant at the table was considered to receive an equal blessing from God in the blessing of the food. As Jesus comes to the party and accepts the place of honor at the banquet, He communicates to the party guests that He counts them as equals.

It would be a tremendous gift for any rabbi to share a meal with those publicly considered sinners and thus communicate with them that they were of equal status as the righteous of their community. But Jesus is no mere rabbi. Jesus is the righteous, holy God of Israel in the flesh. For Him to willingly come and sit at Matthew's table, enjoying the food provided and the company around the table, means something more. Only by God's merciful grace can people come into the presence of the Lord without judgment! As Jesus addresses the Pharisees and their scribes, He brings this truth into focus.

When Jesus hears their complaints, He announces, "Those who are well have no need of a physician, but those who are sick. Go and learn what this means: 'I desire mercy, and not sacrifice.' For I came not to call the righteous, but sinners" (Matthew 9:12–13).

Jesus had come to dine at His newly called disciple's home, and He knew that Matthew would bring other sinners along to the party. Those people needed the grace of forgiveness to heal them from sin and the many deaths sin brings. Sin brings the death of the image of God in which humans were created. It brings the death of relationships as we harm our neighbors and fail to bless them as God intended. Sin brings the death of our place in community, especially for those whose sin is publicly exposed, such as tax collectors. Sin brings relentless physical death as we watch our bodies fail over time and eventually come to a complete halt. Sin brings the eternal death of being completely cut off from our only source of life, which is the Lord Himself. Anyone infected by sin was, and is, in need of Jesus. And Jesus was leading His disciples to recognize their need of Him, the Great Physician.

Anyone infected by sin was, and is, in need of Jesus. And Jesus was leading His disciples to recognize their need of Him, the Great Physician.

Jesus had come to call those who were sick with the disease of sin so that they could come into contact with Him, their cure. By His life, death, and resurrection, Jesus became the only cure for sin. The sinners recognized their need for help. In contrast, Jesus did not come to call the righteous—those who believed they had found some other remedy for sin or believed they were not sinful at all. The Pharisees and scribes didn't think they needed Jesus in the role He had come to fulfill as the Great Physician. Why?

## Mercy and Sacrifice

The Pharisees and scribes would have seen themselves as righteous before God because they had been born into Jewish families, part of God's chosen people. They had received the rite of circumcision on their eighth day of life, bringing them into the covenant of God's promises to His people. From the number of steps they took each Sabbath to their attendance records for every holy day at temple to their tithing records, this group could demonstrate how they had sacrificed on their right path to everlasting life. They had sacrificed by not leading the self-indulgent life Matthew's guests had obviously led. They had sacrificed by rightly keeping the Law of God—or at least their rabbi's interpretation of the Law of God.

They may have known that they needed God's grace for the ways in which they were imperfect, but to have *only* God's grace as their hope for life? This would discount all *they* contributed to their being right with God. This group didn't think they needed Jesus as the sole agent of healing for their broken lives. Through their sacrifices and their families' sacrifices stretching all the way back to Abraham, they had that sin thing taken care of! They simply needed Jesus to fulfill their expectations as a good rabbi. He needed to keep the Law as they did. He needed to submit to their ways, and He certainly needed to avoid contact with sinners! He should have been sticking with them, the righteous ones. And so Jesus acknowledges that, in their own judgment about themselves, they have no apparent need of Him.

This group didn't think they needed Jesus as the sole agent of healing for their broken lives.

Yet even in this pronouncement, I believe Jesus still reveals His heart for this grumbling group when He encourages them to go learn what God means by the phrase "I desire mercy, and not sacrifice" (v. 13).

That phrase—mercy, and not sacrifice—comes from the Old Testament prophet Hosea. Hosea was a prophet in the eighth century BC who proclaimed God's Word amidst rampant idolatry among God's people in the Northern Kingdom of Israel. To illustrate the extent to which the Israelites had walked away from their relationship with their God, Yahweh commanded

His servant Hosea to take an unfaithful wife named Gomer. Gomer may have been unfaithful because she was a prostitute at a pagan temple. (Remember, worship among many ancient pagan religions often included ritualistic sex.)

Here, Jesus quotes a significant point in Hosea's book. Hosea opens chapter 6 with words that seem to come from the people of Israel as they reflect on how far they have drifted from Yahweh. At first, the words seem repentant. They even seem seasoned with overtones of renewal and resurrection. "Come let us return to the Lord. . . . After two days He will revive us; on the third day He will raise us up that we may live before Him" (vv. 1, 2).

Yet the words are mere lip service. The Lord, responding in verses 4–6, expresses His frustration:

> **What shall I do with you, O Ephraim? What shall I do with you, O Judah? Your love is like a morning cloud, like the dew that goes early away. Therefore I have hewn them by the prophets; I have slain them by the words of My mouth, and My judgment goes forth as the light. For I desire steadfast love [mercy] and not sacrifice.**

What is the distinction between steadfast love (mercy) and sacrifice to which Jesus draws the Pharisees' attention at Matthew's banquet? It seems to be a matter of the heart. Let's say that on your anniversary, your spouse gives you a wonderful gift, perhaps your favorite meal or maybe a dozen long-stemmed roses. When you communicate your thanks, suppose your spouse replies, "Honey, you are such a blessing to me! Thank you for the honor of being your spouse all these years." Your spouse has just shown you steadfast love (mercy)—a gift that came from a heart of genuine love for you. However, suppose your spouse interrupts your thanks and says, "Oh, don't bother thanking me. It was our anniversary after all. I was obligated to do something, so I've fulfilled my obligation." Then your spouse has just shown you sacrifice. It may have been the same action, but one comes from a heart of love and the other from a heart cold to the relationship.

God does not desire a loveless obedience that could be reduced to a transactional relationship—"I do what You command. I render to You my sacrifices, and in return, You give me Your favor, oh, and the greatest favor of all, You give me eternal life based on my heartless deeds of submission to Your Law."

God does not desire a loveless obedience that could be reduced to a transactional relationship

Rather, our Lord grants His steadfast love first and freely to those who receive it. That's why Jesus came to earth and to Matthew's home that day: to bring the healing touch of His steadfast love. In fact, the Hebrew word translated as "steadfast love" in Hosea 6 could also be translated as "mercy." Jesus gives healing to those who need God's mercy. This brings a new life of love to the faithful, which then becomes the source of their own response of love to our Lord and to one another. Jesus is at Matthew's table, granting His steadfast love (mercy), the very thing that God desires. Those around the table who, by the Spirit's work, receive Jesus' mercy in faith will find it bearing fruit in their lives in their steadfast love for the Lord and for their neighbors.

This is seen in real time with another tax collector, a guy named Zacchaeus.

## A Tax Collector Despised by Tax Collectors

If you spent any time in Sunday School as a child, you may remember a story (or even a cute "wee little man" song) about a guy named Zacchaeus. What you might not remember is that Zacchaeus and Jesus shared a meal, and that's because it's not explicitly mentioned in the Bible. However, it clearly happened, and the parallels between Zacchaeus's and Matthew's meal encounters with Jesus are why these two men are placed together here.

At the beginning of Luke 19, Jesus is passing through Jericho on His way to Jerusalem. While our Lord knows that He's going to Jerusalem to fulfill His earthly ministry though His Passion, death on the cross, and resurrection, the crowds around Him likely anticipate something far more glorious, at least in earthly terms. Jesus was now well known in the region as a rabbi, prophet, and miracle worker. Was He now heading to Jerusalem to take His rightful place on King David's throne and usher in a new glorious era for Israel? As Jesus makes His way to the holy city with Passover just days away, stories of salvation are hanging in the air.

While our Lord knows that He's going to Jerusalem to fulfill His earthly ministry though His Passion, death on the cross, and resurrection, the crowds around Him likely anticipate something far more glorious.

Crowds would be lining the streets to hail Him, and Jericho would be the last stop before those historic days in Jerusalem.

Zacchaeus was the last person the crowds would expect to share in any good from Jesus. Luke describes Zacchaeus with three significant points. He was the chief tax collector. He was rich. He was short. How do these factors play into his encounter with Jesus?

Nowhere else in the Bible is the term "chief tax collector" used. However, from what we know about tax collectors as noted in Matthew's account above, we can only guess that this meant that Zacchaeus had risen to a supervisory role in a disreputable profession—the chief over those who legally robbed their fellow citizens. What's more, Jericho was a major center for collecting taxes on goods and services since it was located on a major trade route.

I imagine Zacchaeus being a shrewd, hard-knocks kind of guy, someone who knew how to intimidate and extract wealth even from the "unclean" guys who were the type to rob their neighbors. From this enforcer-like position, Zacchaeus had long sold off any hope of being seen as righteous by others. He had most certainly exchanged the chance for eternal salvation through any obedience to God's Law. His consolation prize? Riches!

I expect Zacchaeus used that wealth as a shield. Whenever he felt the sting of being labeled unclean and therefore isolated from the religious community, he would block that feeling by enjoying his wonderful home. Whenever he'd sense the resentment of the people from whom he had stolen, he'd drown out that message with a fine meal and wine. Whenever his own conscience might whisper and remind him that even he didn't like what he was doing, he'd desperately buy something to distract himself.

The final fact Luke shares about Zacchaeus is that he is short. Modern researchers have determined that the human brain uses height as one factor to determine fitness and social status. Men especially are often judged as having less leadership potential, power, and intelligence based on their lack of stature. Scripture doesn't reveal whether Zacchaeus's height played a role in his quest to become a chief tax collector, perhaps wanting to prove wrong those who underestimated him, but it seems possible. His size, however, does play a clear role in his encounter with Jesus.

As Jesus enters Jericho, crowds line the streets to welcome the famous miracle-working prophet. Luke 19:3 tells us that Zacchaeus "was seeking to see who Jesus was," indicating that Zacchaeus was persistent in his efforts. But Zacchaeus could not see over the crowd of onlookers, and as a person looked down on in the community, there was little chance anyone would let him go to the front. Perhaps he even feared standing in front of the crowds because of what they might do to him behind his back.

Still seeking to see Jesus, Zacchaeus does the unthinkable for any respectable first-century Israelite man: he runs ahead of the crowd and climbs a tree. Men in first-century Israel wore long robes and were modest about exposing their skin in public. In order to run, Zacchaeus would have needed to hike up his

Still seeking to see Jesus, Zacchaeus does the unthinkable for any respectable first-century Israelite man: he runs ahead of the crowd and climbs a tree.

robes and expose portions of his legs. Much the same would be true in order for him to climb a tree. Zacchaeus so longed to see Jesus that he does things that would be considered foolish, if not downright humiliating, in his culture.

Yet Zacchaeus is not the only one who is persistently seeking. Jesus says that He, too, has been earnestly seeking. He came to seek and to save the lost. And that's why "when Jesus came to the place, He looked up and said to him, 'Zacchaeus, hurry and come down, for I must stay at your house today.' So he hurried and came down and received Him joyfully" (vv. 5–6).

## The Place Where Jesus Abides

This account may give the impression that Jesus is merely inviting Himself to lodge at what was likely the nicest home in Jericho. Another way of translating Jesus' statement may help clarify that something far greater is happening. Jesus said, "Zacchaeus, hurry and come down, for this day in your house it is necessary for Me to abide" (v. 5, my own translation).

Why is it necessary for Jesus to abide in Zacchaeus's home on that very day? Because if Jesus does not abide in his home, then Jesus will not find and save the lost there, namely Zacchaeus himself. But if Jesus does abide there, He brings the gift of God's merciful love and forgiveness to those who also abide there. Jesus brings the gift of salvation and eternal life, a gift He will purchase at the cost of His own life on the cross, which is why He's on His way to Jerusalem.

If Jesus does abide there, He brings the gift of God's merciful love and forgiveness to those who also abide there.

The same is true for us all. If Jesus does not abide with us, we are lost in sin and death. Therefore, our Lord sees the urgent need and says He must abide with Zacchaeus and likewise with us. He does so by the work of the Spirit through His Word and the daily renewal of His baptismal covenant with us. As Jesus abides with us, salvation comes to us as well!

Zacchaeus responds by joyfully receiving Jesus into his home. Here is where the dinner is implied in the text! No one in first-century Israel would receive someone into their home and not provide a meal. Holding a meal in Jesus' honor would not only fulfill the cultural expectations of hospitality on Zacchaeus's part, but it would also reflect the forgiving grace Jesus had brought into Zacchaeus's life by becoming a guest in his home.

Like the crowd that looked on at Matthew's party at the start of Jesus' ministry, the crowd in Jericho also looks on in shocked offense. The crowd labels Zacchaeus a sinner, but their grumbling that Jesus has gone to be his guest is really a complaint against Jesus' rash behavior in prompting the invitation.

Yet Zacchaeus's response is the fruit of faith. Zacchaeus stands and declares, "Behold, Lord, the half of my goods I give to the poor. And if I have defrauded anyone of anything, I restore it fourfold" (v. 8). His statement may reflect that he is aware of what God's Word says in Exodus 22:1 and 2 Samuel 12:5–6 about making restoration to those from whom one has stolen. He is repentant of sin, and in Jesus' forgiving grace, Zacchaeus is already beginning to live out his faith in Jesus.

Zacchaeus no longer needs his ill-gotten wealth to shield him from the disdain of his community and the label of unclean.

He has the grace of Jesus and, with it, a wealth of life beyond anything he could acquire by his former ways! Jesus puts it beautifully when He says, "Today salvation has come to this house, since he also is a son of Abraham. For the Son of Man came to seek and to save the lost" (vv. 9–10). Zacchaeus is a son of Abraham, for he received by faith the same Messiah whom Abraham also trusted for salvation.

It is no mistake that the events of Jesus' incarnate ministry are somewhat bookended by fellowship meals with reputed sinners. In both Matthew's and Zacchaeus's encounters with the Messiah, Jesus extends a gracious invitation. There is an immediate, joyful response. There is a celebration meal where the Savior is the guest of honor and an outside crowd that murmurs, objecting to Jesus' fellowship practices. Yet the Messiah is not dissuaded from His mission, of which these tax collectors are a part.

Jesus sits down to dine with sinners while they are still sinners.

Jesus sits down to dine with sinners while they are still sinners. But before the final course is finished, Jesus has brought them to repentance and granted His blood-bought gift of salvation. Can anything different be said when our Lord graciously invites us to dine at His Holy Table?

## QUESTIONS FOR DESSERT

What things do people hold to today as a way to consider themselves righteous and in no need of Jesus' healing grace? What things do you hold to rather than Jesus?

______________________________________________

______________________________________________

______________________________________________

______________________________________________

______________________________________________

How does being freely welcomed to Christ's table address our ways of justifying ourselves?

______________________________________________

______________________________________________

______________________________________________

______________________________________________

______________________________________________

What people might be considered "unclean" in your community? How might Jesus use you to welcome them to Himself?

______________________________________________

______________________________________________

______________________________________________

______________________________________________

______________________________________________

Chapter 6

# WHEN GOD DROPS IN FOR DINNER

*But Martha was distracted with much serving.*

— LUKE 10:40 —

**WHAT ARE THE OBLIGATIONS, THE** social expectations of hospitality, for the modern American home if someone unexpectedly shows up for a visit? It's a trick question because in our current times, very rarely does someone visit unannounced! The practice of showing up without warning to a friend or relative's home has been on the decline for years.

There was a time in American culture when welcoming unplanned guests was common and accepted, and those times brought different expectations for hospitality. If someone dropped in on friends or family, even less socially adept hosts would meet some basic standards of welcome—putting on a pot of coffee or tea, having some pastries or snacks at the ready in case company popped by, and offering them the best chair.

If the person came by close to mealtime, extra food would be prepared and an extra place would be set at the table. Some families even had a room reserved for entertaining guests, even if those guests came by without invitation. Sometimes that room's furniture was covered in plastic slip covers to keep it clean for guests (or perhaps to keep the guest's stay a little shorter). We still enjoy friends and community today, but it does seem that there used to be a higher sense of obligation to welcome an unexpected visitor.

We still enjoy friends and community today, but it does seem that there used to be a higher sense of obligation to welcome an unexpected visitor.

Today, many regard an impromptu visitor as anything from a nuisance to downright rude. It's more than the expectation someone should be able to at least shoot you a text before arriving on the "Welcome" or "No soliciting" mat at your front door. We've come to think differently about our homes in general. Our homes have become retreat centers, places to get away from it all by sealing ourselves in our garage-connected, climate-controlled, video-doorbelled fortresses of solitude. "A man's home is his castle" might have been the slogan of a bygone era, but now that castle's moat is filled with alligators, and the drawbridge is pulled up. If someone is so bold as to breach the perimeter of our homes and get through the front door, we'll extend some basic kindnesses, but probably in the hopes that such graces will be rewarded with an incredibly brief stay. The longer the guest lingers, the more likely we are to send subtle, perhaps even subconscious signals that we'd like to get on with our plans for the day—which did not include being hospitable to our self-invited friend.

It may be a response to how busy and overscheduled our lives can become. Perhaps it's a reaction to the rise of our self-selected (and therefore seemingly more controlled) virtual community of social media, which seems to easily find its way into our fortresses. This endless stream of virtual content may leave us unavailable for in-person anything, even the pop-by visit of a friend. Whatever the reasons, we tend not to consider our homes a resource to welcome others and create community for those who come, invited or uninvited.

However, that was not the case in first-century Israel!

## Welcoming Jesus to Your Home

At the beginning of Luke 10, Jesus sends seventy-two of His disciples to prepare the towns Jesus was about to visit. They are to heal the sick and proclaim the message that the kingdom of God has come near. Jesus instructs them to graciously accept invitations to stay with people who welcome them into their homes in those towns, "eating and drinking what they provide" (v. 7). It was common practice to open your doors to welcome new people who arrived in a village, even for days on end. Jesus' disciples would experience this as they prepared the various towns and villages for Jesus' arrival. When the disciples return, having finished their preparatory work, Jesus begins His follow-up journey. Luke tells us that "Jesus entered a village. And a woman named Martha welcomed Him into her house. And she had a sister called Mary" (vv. 38–39).

If these are the same Mary and Martha mentioned in John 11, we know a few things about them. They develop a close, loving relationship with Jesus as His faithful followers. Mary is the woman who anoints Jesus and wipes His feet with her hair. These sisters have a brother, Lazarus, whom Jesus will raise from the dead toward the end of His earthly ministry. That is when Martha makes the powerful confession to Jesus just before her brother is raised, "Yes, Lord; I believe that You are the Christ, the Son of God, who is coming into the world" (John 11:27).

Luke's account of the encounter at Martha and Mary's home does not mention who all was part of Jesus' traveling party. However, it's likely that Martha opens her home not only to Jesus but also to His twelve main disciples, and perhaps even some of the seventy-two disciples who may have accompanied them. For Martha to show hospitality, then, would entail more than preparing one extra place setting at the table. She may have found herself unexpectedly hosting a large dinner party.

She may have found herself unexpectedly hosting a large dinner party.

Offering hospitality to a large group—even if the main guest happens to be God Incarnate—may seem like the most surprising thing about this visit to modern American sensibilities. But early readers of Luke would have been shocked by two other things: that a first-century Israelite woman is doing the welcoming and that Jesus, a first-century Jewish rabbi, actually accepts her hospitality. More than that, Jesus enters her home and teaches, which would have been unheard of! Something even more shocking happens as Martha's sister, Mary, enters the picture.

## Tension with a Sister or with God?

Martha begins preparing to serve their guests. But as Jesus begins to teach, Mary boldly breaks a cultural barrier and places herself at His feet. Normally, only the men would listen to and engage with the rabbi, and the women might catch a few morsels of the teaching content while they prepared the meal. Rather than fulfilling her culturally expected role as a woman, Mary assumes a place among the male disciples and listens to what Jesus has to say.

Have you ever noticed that when someone in a group steps out of his or her lane and behaves in an unexpected way, others in the group can get stressed out or even angry? I wonder what was going through Martha's mind as her sister overstepped those cultural boundaries. Perhaps Martha worried for their reputation as godly women or feared what other barriers Mary might try to break. Luke tells us that Martha felt burdened by preparing everything for their guests without her sister's help. While Mary sat at Jesus' feet and listened to His teaching, Martha was literally "dragged around" with all the serving duties of hosting others.[3] I can imagine Martha darting about their home, first bringing out water, then maybe some wineskins or fruit for the guests, glancing at her sister and signaling for help each time she entered the room, her internal tension building.

At some point in the evening, Martha can hold back those frustrated thoughts no longer. While she may have wanted to be a proper and gracious host and fulfill the expectation of

3 See the textual note on Luke 10:40 in Arthur A. Just Jr., *Luke 9:51–24:53*, Concordia Commentary (Concordia Publishing House, 1997), 457.

hospitality, she now does a very inhospitable thing. She engages her guest of honor to rule on a family dispute. She goes up to Jesus and says, "Lord, do You not care that my sister has left me to serve alone? Tell her then to help me" (Luke 10:40).

> While she may have wanted to be a proper and gracious host and fulfill the expectation of hospitality, she now does a very inhospitable thing.

Martha may truly have valued showing hospitality. It's a virtue held up time and again in the New Testament. Peter encourages Christians to "show hospitality to one another without grumbling" (1 Peter 4:9). In Titus 1:8, Paul lists hospitality as a qualification for serving as an elder (pastor) of the church. Paul encourages all Christians to show hospitality in Romans 12:13. The author of Hebrews goes so far as to say, "Do not neglect to show hospitality to strangers, for thereby some have entertained angels unawares" (13:2). So Martha, in wanting to be a good host, is not seeking something displeasing to God.

The trouble seems to be that Martha holds too traditional of an understanding of what it means to show hospitality. She equates showing hospitality with providing food for her guests. In Martha's mind, Mary's choice to sit at Jesus' feet was in essence neglecting their guests' needs. It was rude to their guests and especially to Martha, as she was left alone to complete all the duties. In appealing to Jesus, she expects that He will see things her way as well.

## The Many Ways of Hospitality

Jesus' response shows Martha a different perspective. Martha does not recognize that Mary is also exercising a true form of hospitality. When a guest comes to proclaim the Word of God, it is hospitable to welcome him or her by providing for temporal needs, such as a refreshing drink and a meal. But it is even more hospitable to honor the guest's teaching by humbly sitting and listening to what he or she has come to say. Martha's view of hospitality led her to be dragged away from Jesus' teaching by the many distractions of serving. Mary's practice of hospitality led her to the only thing needed: listening to the words of Jesus.

When Martha appeals to Him, Jesus lovingly chides her, "Martha, Martha, you are anxious and troubled about many things, but one thing is necessary. Mary has chosen the good portion, which will not be taken away from her" (Luke 10:41–42). Martha is concerned about serving food, so Jesus plays on her concern by speaking of the "good portion" that Mary has chosen. With His teaching, Jesus is serving a feast to those who sit in the room and listen; that is the good portion. Martha is troubled about the many details of serving as a gracious host to her guests. Jesus contrasts her trouble over many things with Mary's concern over the one thing necessary: hearing His Word of the gift of God's forgiving love, which is the heart of Jesus' teaching and the very reason He came into the world.

With His teaching, Jesus is serving a feast to those who sit in the room and listen; that is the good portion.

The gift of Jesus' Gospel is the one thing needed because by it our Lord gives life that lasts eternally. A good meal, even one delivered with the warmest of hospitality, will only sustain its recipients for a short while. But what Jesus gave in Martha's house that day and gives to us today will sustain all who receive it even beyond death to life everlasting. That gift transcends time, tradition, and cultural expectations. So, Mary need not dash off to do some lesser thing, even if it is the good thing of serving Jesus food. Mary was receiving the one thing needed because Jesus served her the good portion of His grace, which He would pay for with His precious blood, and that portion would never be taken from her.

We do not know what happened after Jesus' statement. Did Martha, now lovingly corrected by Jesus, put down her cooking utensils and join her sister and the others at Jesus' feet? Did Mary attentively wait for Jesus to finish His teaching then joyfully respond to Christ's message by helping Martha prepare a meal? Perhaps Luke doesn't share how the situation concluded because Jesus' statement during this encounter was so significant. While Martha believed she was hosting Jesus that day, He was the true host. He came to her home not to be served by Martha and Mary but to serve them and all in their home with His message of God's love. Jesus did not need their hospitality; they needed His. And He gives the good portion in full measure.

Jesus did not need their hospitality; they needed His. And He gives the good portion in full measure.

It's easy to identify with Martha. In the rush of our lives, it can seem like we hardly have time to feed ourselves, much less provide a gracious meal to unexpected guests. We might even feel the same self-pitying twinge of frustration as Martha when serving our Lord by caring for His followers—especially if others seem blissfully unoccupied with such service. We might hear our own voice added to Martha's: "Lord, don't You care? Tell the others to help me!"

Fortunately, our Lord meets us with the same gentle, corrective love He showed Martha. It may seem like the most important thing to do when Jesus draws near is serve Him—to give our offerings, feed the poor, care for the elderly, volunteer to assist with worship, and so on. These are good things! But here is the true rhythm of hospitality: when Jesus comes near to us, He first comes to serve you and me. He is the one who warmly welcomes us into His presence. He first gives us what we need in the gift of His grace and forgiveness. He is the one who first rejoices to find us at His table to receive what He has prepared for us. The first order of our hospitality back to Jesus is to joyfully sit at His feet, listen to Him, and, in so doing, feast on the meal He freely provides.

We may not find many unexpected guests at our door—probably much to our relief. But should that guest just drop by, show him or her the full hospitality of feeding his or her body and soul. Take the time to truly listen and grow in relationship as you eat together. The Lord may open the door for you to share the one thing needed with that person or for him or her to share that good portion with you.

## QUESTIONS FOR DESSERT

Do you think of yourself more as a Martha or a Mary kind of person? Why is that true for you?

How can even good things in your life drag you away from sitting at Jesus' feet?

When tempted to compare others' level of service to the Lord with your own, what tempers that temptation for you?

Who needs a full, hospitable welcome to your table? How will Jesus be there when it happens?

Chapter 7

# FEEDING THOUSANDS

*They need not go away; you give them something to eat.*

— MATTHEW 14:16 —

**THEY CONVERGED ON MILWAUKEE IN** late June of 2023. Nearly four thousand women and men came from around the world. They came to celebrate Christ's grace in their lives, to grow in their faith through worship and Bible study, and to fellowship in what felt like an extended family reunion. These followers of Christ also came to pledge their continuing support for the mission of the church throughout the world, raising millions in offerings by putting spare change in small purple boxes. It was the fortieth biennial convention of the Lutheran Women's Missionary League! And while the meals probably weren't the main reason for anyone to attend, these convention-goers also came to eat.

One of the convention planners shared what it took to provide food for this group of thousands. Some 825 pounds of pork loin was served at Friday's dinner. Approximately 865 pounds of beef sirloin was served at Saturday's. And they served 675 pounds of popcorn during the convention! To serve these hungry crowds, the convention center deployed a staff of 103 servers, 27 culinary team members, 14 managers, and 10 meal supervisors. It takes detailed planning and a great deal of effort to host meals for such large groups. And the numbers here don't even factor in the infrastructure that made such a meal possible—the farmers, meat workers, truck drivers, refrigerator makers, power-plant workers, and so on who played some small role in delivering those meals.

Can you imagine facing a much larger, hungrier crowd in the wilderness knowing you only have the resources for a small lunch for one? In first-century Israel, that impossible situation happened twice!

Can you imagine facing a much larger, hungrier crowd in the wilderness knowing you only have the resources for a small lunch for one?

## Setting the Scene for the Feast

"Now when Jesus heard this, He withdrew from there in a boat to a desolate place by Himself. But when the crowds heard it, they followed Him on foot from the towns" (Matthew 14:13). What had Jesus heard that moved Him to withdraw to a desolate place?

News of Jesus' growing fame had reached the ears of King Herod, and news of King Herod's recent dealings with John the Baptist had reached the ears of Jesus. John the Baptist was a force to be reckoned with, even for the heads of state. As the forerunner of the Messiah, John had followers as far away as Ephesus—over six hundred miles from Jerusalem—decades after his prophetic ministry came to its abrupt end. Many wondered whether John himself were the Messiah. John flatly denied such claims. Yet it's little wonder such speculation swirled as the crowds flocked to the Jordan River to hear a powerful, if eccentric, wilderness preacher and receive a Baptism of repentance for forgiveness of sins. In pointing people to the One who was to follow him, John spoke the truth of God's Word, even when that truth was uncomfortable to hear. Such was the case for King Herod.

Herod Antipas ruled in Galilee and the region called Perea, just east of the Jordan River, where John's ministry took place. Herod had been married to Phasaelis, but he divorced her to marry Herodias, his half-brother's wife. While staying as a guest in the home of his half-brother, Herod persuaded Herodias to leave her husband for him. Such actions would likely not raise eyebrows today, but it was extremely scandalous in first-century Israel.

As the Lord's prophet, John knew well that the Lord had prohibited what Herod had done. In Leviticus 18:16, Moses had written, "You shall not uncover the nakedness of your brother's wife; it is your brother's nakedness." John boldly condemned the actions of this ruler, publicly calling out his sin. Herod had a mixed view of John. He wanted to kill him but feared the potential backlash from the people who supported this wildly popular prophet. He also regarded John as a righteous and holy man, and he gladly heard him preach. So, to silence John's condemnation of him, Herod had him imprisoned.

However, imprisoning John wasn't enough in the eyes of Herodias. Mark 6:19 records that "Herodias had a grudge against him and wanted to put him to death," but Herod wasn't convinced. Herodias sought an opportunity to force Herod's hand in the matter. That opportunity came on the occasion of Herod's birthday, when Herod threw himself a party. Herodias's daughter Salome performed a provocative dance for him and his guests. The dance pleased Herod so much that he promised the girl whatever she wanted, up to half of his kingdom, on oath before his guests—high officials, military commanders, and leading men of Galilee. Advised by her mother, Salome asked for the head of John the Baptist on a platter! Herod was distressed by the request, but not wanting to look like he wasn't a man of his word before his guests, he gave the order, and John was beheaded.

## A Turning Point in Jesus' Mission

A report is brought to Jesus of the execution of John, His relative. That's the news He receives that causes Him to withdraw with His closest disciples to a solitary place. They sail to the northeast side of the Sea of Galilee to the area near the fishing village of Bethsaida.

Mark tells us that Jesus withdraws because the press of the crowds was such that He and His apostles didn't even have a chance to eat. With the added sad news of John's death, Jesus wants them to have a break, perhaps to grieve and reflect on John's work to prepare people for the Messiah. It's also likely that Jesus deliberately chooses the location for His first actions in His post-John-the-Baptizer ministry, which would culminate with a massive meal. With everything on the table, Jesus takes the apostles and withdraws to a solitary place.

Their solitude is short-lived. When the crowd sees that Jesus and His apostles are leaving by boat, the people scramble on foot to go with them. The situation develops rapidly as the word spreads: the great prophet and miracle worker is leaving, and if you want the blessing of being with Him, there's no time to lose! The people make no provision for themselves and their journey but simply join the crowd making its way to where Jesus will be. I imagine nearby villages looking like ghost towns just a short time after Jesus' boat leaves, as everyone dashes after Him.

The people make no provision for themselves and their journey but simply join the crowd making its way to where Jesus will be.

But as the boat docks and Jesus sees the crowds waiting for Him, He does not lament that His plans to rest are thwarted. He does not angrily send the crowds away. They are His creatures in need of Him. Moved at the gut for them, Jesus responds with compassion. The Gospel writers tell us that Jesus spends the day with this mass of people, healing those who are diseased and teaching the people God's Word and about His reign in their lives.

The crowd is in awe as Jesus moves among them, speaking the wisdom of His Word and healing their loved ones. As evening approaches, a practical matter comes to the thoughts of Jesus' closest followers: food. The disciples assess the situation and come to Jesus with a solution. "This is a desolate place, and the day is now over; send the crowds away to go into the villages and buy food for themselves," they say (Matthew

14:15). This is not a cold or foolish suggestion on the part of the disciples. The crowds are not in some great crisis. At best, they've only been a day without a meal. Also, they're in a desolate place—there are no practical means to produce a meal. The surrounding towns and villages seem the best option to handle the need. The disciples are genuinely attempting to address the need at the moment with the best solution they can imagine. Of course, they are forgetting who is in their midst!

Jesus puts a challenge to them: "They need not go away; you give them something to eat" (v. 16). The disciples speculate how much it would cost them to buy everyone some bread, and they seem to ascertain from a quick search that one boy among them has five barley loaves (think dinner rolls) and two fish. Jesus' words invite us to ponder why He chose to involve His disciples when He already knew He would produce a miraculous meal for them. But with that instruction, Jesus involves His disciples in the work of His kingdom. It's a rhythm the disciples will see in their ministry throughout their lives. Jesus does not need His disciples to accomplish His will, but in His grace, He will still use them far beyond their actual means of serving.

Jesus does not need His disciples to accomplish His will, but in His grace, He will still use them far beyond their actual means of serving.

## Seeing the Bigger Picture

Yet couldn't that ministry lesson have been learned by the disciples as they helped manage the crowd and Jesus taught and healed people in the crowd? If the crowd had gone into the surrounding towns for a meal per the disciples' plan, the disciples still would have learned an important ministry lesson. The crowds still would have gone away with Jesus' instruction in God's Word, teachings about His reign in their lives, and the gift of healing for their loved ones. Why does Jesus bother with the added miracle of feeding them with the completely inadequate means that the disciples found?

Besides the miracle of Jesus' resurrection on Easter, the feeding of the five thousand is the only other miracle recorded in all four Gospels. Clearly these authors saw it as an important event in Jesus' ministry. Their accounts give some clues as to why Jesus chose to work this miracle and why it was so important.

Jesus instructs the disciples to have the people sit down together in groups of fifties and hundreds. Such detail brings to mind how the Lord instructed Moses to organize the people of Israel while they were journeying to the Promised Land. Moses was to appoint leaders over groups of people; Exodus 18:21 specifically mentions groups of hundreds and fifties. Moses was God's promised deliverer who led the people from a desolate place to the Promised Land. Here, Jesus shows Himself as the greater deliverer who has come to do the same, as John the Baptist had been preaching about Him.

Here, Jesus shows Himself as the greater deliverer who has come to the do the same.

The instruction to sit in larger groups might also touch on a matter of mealtime fellowship. In first-century Israel, it was customary to eat only with people whom you knew well and considered your equals, if not as close as family. Among this teeming mass of people—some five thousand men, plus any women and children—what is the likelihood that everyone in each group considered everyone else in the group as close as family? In other words, this crowd's mealtime fellowship will not be based on their social customs. They are to fellowship in a meal based solely on their common connection to the host, Jesus, and His miraculous provision of food. This reflects the fellowship of the church, where we are brought together into a community and fellowship based on our common connection to Christ, our Savior, and not on any cultural customs.

With the crowd organized and seated, Jesus feeds them. Jesus' actions with the loaves and fish reflect the spiritual traditions of a typical first-century Israelite meal. He takes the food; looks up to heaven, reminding the partakers of the meal that these gifts come from the heavenly Father; and gives thanks to His Father. He then breaks the food into pieces and gives it to the people.

The expressions the Gospel writers use to describe Jesus' actions here are also used to describe Jesus' postresurrection meal at Emmaus (more on that later) and, more significantly, His institution of the Lord's Supper (more on that later too!). Early Christians regularly used the image of the loaves and fish from this miracle as a symbol for Holy Communion. The loaves were a reminder of God's provision of manna in the wilderness, and the fish came to be associated with Christ Himself. The letters that make up the Greek word for "fish," ICHTHUS, were used as a confessional acronym for "Jesus Christ, God's Son, Savior." In the Gospel of John, the feeding of the five thousand comes just before Jesus reveals that He is the bread of life, and the dialogue that follows in John 6 has strong Communion overtones.

The result of Jesus' actions with the loaves and fish? Thousands are fed and fully satisfied, with even more left over than when they started! Jesus instructs the disciples to gather the leftover pieces, and they collect twelve basketfuls. Was this Jesus blessing each of the Twelve with a feast for themselves after the crowds had been served? Or was this a powerful lesson to them that Jesus would fully supply them each for all the work He would have them do in bringing others into His kingdom? However the disciples received it, the miracle revealed Jesus as the abundant provider of that which sustains life in its fullness, even with limited means, even in a desolate place!

The miracle revealed Jesus as the abundant provider of that which sustains life in its fullness, even with limited means, even in a desolate place!

## Feeding Thousands, Gentile Style

Since He had just worked the miracle of feeding over five thousand people, it may seem odd for Jesus to conduct another miraculous feeding of a large crowd a short while later. Yet Matthew and Mark record just such an event, this time with four thousand people. Did these two evangelists simply get things confused and discuss the same miracle meal twice? Some may think so, but Jesus Himself distinguishes the two miraculous meals (see Matthew 16:9–10), and the miracle of the feeding of the four thousand is distinct in its context, details, and potential lessons Jesus teaches through it.

Not long before the miracle of the feeding of the four thousand, Matthew and Mark record that the Pharisees confront Jesus over His disciples' behavior. They accuse the disciples of breaking with the tradition of the elders by eating with unwashed hands. The Pharisees value being ceremonially clean as a sign of being clean in God's eyes, so they are really accusing Jesus' disciples (and thus Jesus as their leader) of dismissing the need to be clean in God's eyes. While Jesus rebukes the Pharisees as hypocrites for holding to the traditions of men over God's commands, He uses the controversy to help His disciples consider what truly makes someone clean in God's eyes. Jesus teaches them that what comes from a person's heart—sin—is what makes someone unclean to God. This sets up how the disciples will be challenged in their view of Gentiles both in the encounter that immediately follows and in the next feeding miracle.

After this discussion, Jesus takes the disciples to the Gentile region near the city of Tyre. There, a Canaanite woman begs Him to heal her daughter, who is possessed by an evil spirit. Jesus' disciples ask Him to give her what she wants so that she'll leave them alone (it seems the disciples' solution to problems is "Send them away"). But Jesus chooses to teach them through this situation. He declares that there is a priority in His ministry for the lost sheep of the house of Israel, as He was sent for them. Yet He reveals that God's abundance will overflow to the Gentiles as well, and He does

He reveals that God's abundance will overflow to the Gentiles as well, and He does so through a meal analogy.

so through a meal analogy. The brief exchange between Jesus and the Canaanite woman at this point is powerful:

> **But she came and knelt before Him, saying, "Lord, help me." And He answered, "It is not right to take the children's bread and throw it to the dogs." She said, "Yes, Lord, yet even the dogs eat the crumbs that fall from their master's table." Then Jesus answered her, "O woman, great is your faith! Be it done for you as you desire." And her daughter was healed instantly.** (Matthew 15:25–28)

Jesus has now taught the disciples that what makes someone clean or unclean in God's eyes is the sin of a person's heart, not the human traditions they kept or their ethnic background. The disciples also witness Jesus marvel at the faith of a Gentile woman, as He allows the crumbs of His healing grace to fall into her life, cleansing her daughter of a demon that had possessed her. Things are set for their master to allow abundant crumbs to fall from His table once again, only now to feed a very different crowd.

In transition, Matthew records that Jesus healed many people. Mark draws his readers' focus to just one healing of someone who was deaf and mute. Both accounts give us a full picture of the crowds now following Jesus. Matthew says the crowds praise "the god of Israel" as they witness the many healings performed by Jesus. This indicates that many, if not most, of the people in the crowd are not Israelites; they are Gentiles. Mark tells us that these healings take place in the region of the Decapolis, an area mostly populated by Gentiles. Again this suggests that the crowd about to be fed by Jesus is mostly made up of Gentiles.

We now come to Jesus' second miraculous meal! While there are certainly details in this miracle that parallel the feeding of the five thousand, there are also notable distinctions. Rather than being with Jesus for a day like the five thousand, this crowd has been following Jesus for three days. During the feeding of the five thousand, the disciples seemed to initiate the conversation about feeding the crowd. Here, it is Jesus who initiates the conversation about feeding them. He calls His disciples over and says, "I have compassion on the crowd because they have been with Me now three days and have nothing to eat. And I am unwilling to send them away hungry, lest they faint on the way" (Matthew 15:32).

The disciples' response to Jesus is also quite different with this miracle. Now, rather than trying to figure it out themselves or wanting the crowd to find their own solution to their hunger, the disciples simply ponder in general where they are going to get enough bread in a desolate place to feed such a crowd. Perhaps, remembering the first miracle meal, they are already anticipating that Jesus will again be the solution.

Perhaps, remembering the first miracle meal, they are already anticipating that Jesus will again be the solution.

Jesus asks what bread supply they have, and the disciples indicate they have seven loaves and a few small fish. Now the miracle bears a striking resemblance to the first. Having directed the crowd to take a seat, Jesus follows the same method of giving thanks to God, breaking the meal elements into pieces, and giving them to the disciples to give to the people. Both groups—one primarily Jewish, one likely Gentile—will be fed in the same way by the same Messiah in their midst.

Like the crowd of five thousand, the crowd of four thousand eat to the point of satisfaction, and there is an abundance left over. This time, the disciples gather seven baskets full. The term translated here as "basket" indicates a much larger container than the ones used at the feeding of the five thousand. In the Bible, the number *7* often symbolizes completion, as God rested from all His work of creation on the seventh day of creation. Perhaps this detail with the seven containers shows Jesus' disciples that He would fully supply them as they do their work of bringing the Good News of God's gracious reign until it was brought to completion among the Gentiles.

Both miraculous meals occurred in remote, solitary places, yet Jesus was there. So in reality, they were full of life. As crowds follow Him, bringing along people who are sick and who cannot walk, Jesus provides to the full! He heals. He teaches the Good News of the reign of God in the lives of His people. Then, He offers a meal. He provides more than a snack to get them on their way. These meals represent a new community being formed—one centered on Christ and gathered around His Word, one where His compassion addresses their needs. It's a community where Jew and Gentile alike share in Jesus' same blessing.

These meals represent a new community being formed—one centered on Christ and gathered around His Word.

That community is still found today. It's being taught God's Word, cared for by His compassionate grace, and fed a miraculous meal under the blessing of the same Jesus who fed the five thousand and the four thousand. Jesus' provision is still enough to fully meet the needs of all who come, including your family and you!

## QUESTIONS FOR DESSERT

Take a moment to review what we ask of our Lord when we pray, "Give us this day our daily bread." What are all the ways Jesus provides for your temporal life each day?

Which daily provision of God in your life have you been especially thankful for recently?

What added blessings does our Lord give when He feeds us in group settings rather than as individuals? How does this shape our understanding of life together as Christians?

CHAPTER 8

# ANOINTED BY A SINNER, FORGIVEN BY THE SAVIOR

*Do you see this woman?*

— LUKE 7:44 —

## Getting a Get!

**IF YOU WERE GOING TO** hold an epic dinner party, who would make your list as a "get" attendee? Could you imagine if your party had a music theme and Taylor Swift said she'd come, or if the party had a movie theme and Tom Hanks checked the yes box on his RSVP? Sometimes people invite famous people to their proms or weddings with the slim hopes that they'll actually come. When they do, it usually makes the news. While they didn't extend the invite, I think my son-in-law would have been just slightly more joyful had LeBron James shown up for his and my daughter's wedding! And quite frankly, Brandon Flowers or Ryan Reynolds, if you're reading this, swing by my place anytime for dinner.

The internet is filled with stories about top-shelf celebrities charging millions of dollars to perform at private parties, but some people will pay extravagant sums for a famous person simply to show up at their soiree as a guest. Think of your ideal dinner party get. Would you be willing to pay him or her just to come? Would you tell the other guests that person was coming, or would you wait and let them be surprised as the celebrity strolls through the door? More important, how would you treat such a get while he or she is in your home and at your table?

A religious leader named Simon got the get of all gets to attend his dinner party—God Incarnate, Jesus!

A religious leader named Simon got the get of all gets to attend his dinner party—God Incarnate, Jesus! However, an unwanted guest crashed the party and received something far greater than the bragging rights of hosting a famous guest.

People the world over today identify Jesus as one of history's most famous and influential persons, and of course, His followers joyfully confess Him to be Lord and Savior. But His true identity wasn't so apparent during His incarnate life in first-century Israel. During His three-year ministry, He was known by crowds as a powerful preacher who taught God's Word with authority (unlike the other rabbis of the day). Stories of His ability to do the miraculous, even healings and casting out demons, spread like wildfire. His willingness to associate with the lowly and outcast of society and some of

His more controversial teachings sometimes seemed to place Him at odds with the religious leaders of the day. Jesus' words and actions compelled people to form conclusions about who He really was, and those conclusions varied wildly.

The uncertainty over Jesus' identity even seems to have touched the heart of His forerunner, John the Baptist. Just before the account of Simon's dinner party in Luke 7, John, languishing in King Herod's dungeon, hears reports of all that Jesus is saying and doing. He sends two of his own disciples to ask Jesus, "Are You the one who is to come, or shall we look for another?" (v. 19).

It may be that Jesus did not necessarily look like the Messiah John had been proclaiming. John had preached that the coming Messiah would bring judgment against the unrepentant, as he told some religious leaders who came out to his Baptism:

> **You brood of vipers! Who warned you to flee from the wrath to come? . . . Even now the axe is laid to the root of the trees. Every tree therefore that does not bear good fruit is cut down and thrown into the fire. . . . His winnowing fork is in His hand, and He will clear His threshing floor and gather His wheat into the barn, but the chaff He will burn with unquenchable fire.** (Matthew 3:7, 10, 12)

Jesus' ministry was hallmarked by compassion and mercy. John, possibly anticipating that his days are numbered, may have had doubts about Jesus' true identity, so he sends some disciples to seek confirmation from Jesus Himself.

As John's disciples come with his question, they witness Jesus' ministry in action as He heals many people. He then sends them back to John with a message that lists His acts of mercy, chiefly that "the poor have good news preached to them" (Luke 7:22). No one, including John the Baptist, should fall away from Jesus on account of His earthly ministry because that ministry is a fulfillment of the Old Testament messianic prophecies. His coming role as judge will be fulfilled only after His mission as Savior is completed.

His coming role as judge will be fulfilled only after His mission as Savior is completed.

As John's disciples leave, Jesus tells the crowds that John is a prophet and even more than a prophet: "I tell you, among those born of women none is greater than John. Yet the one who is least in the kingdom of God is greater than he" (v. 28). I can imagine the crowds who had followed John wondering, "Just who is Jesus to speak with such authority about the great prophet John?" Those who rejected John and his Baptism also must consider Jesus' identity, and one Pharisee named Simon will get the chance to ponder that point in his own home.

## Entering Simon's House

Many rabbis in the days of Jesus' earthly ministry believed that the Spirit of God had departed from Israel nearly four hundred fifty years before, with the close of the prophet Malachi's ministry. Since that time, there had been no more prophetic word from the Lord. Now Jesus sparks a debate among the spiritual leaders of Israel. Some leaders held Jesus to be a prophet, and Jesus Himself had already declared He was a prophet in Luke 4:24. The Pharisee Nicodemus tells Jesus, "We know that You are a teacher come from God, for no one can do these signs that You do unless God is with him" (John 3:2). Other leaders, however, rejected the notion that Jesus was from God and believed quite the opposite, teaching that Jesus performed His miracles by the power of the devil instead. A Pharisee named Simon will now draw his own conclusions about Jesus as Jesus and Simon dine at Simon's table.

But how did Jesus get invited to Simon's for dinner in the first place? The dinner party recorded in Luke 7:36–50 was likely a festive meal called a Chaburah, a Sabbath evening Seder. Simon may have heard Jesus preach at a local synagogue earlier that day. Perhaps he wanted to continue the conversation with this possible new prophet from God as his guest of honor. Or maybe Simon also wanted the chance to offer some correctives to the new rabbi. Jesus had been teaching that the Lord loves sinners; the Pharisees taught that God loves the righteous—those who fulfill the Law by their obedience. A dinner conversation might allow Simon to judge for himself Jesus' bona fides as a prophet and bring this young rabbi from Galilee into greater wisdom on whom God truly loves.

However, there may also have been a darker motive behind Simon's invitation to Jesus. The Pharisees had been watching Jesus closely in the hopes of catching Him in some teaching or act that would warrant His arrest. Many religious leaders feared making such a bold move against Jesus, knowing that the general population viewed Him as a prophet. What better way to build a case against Him than to welcome Him with seeming honor in the hopes that He would slip up at a well-attended party where He's the keynote guest? At this particular party, Jesus will offer even more reason for the religious leaders to justify their rejection and ultimate condemnation of Him, while at the same time offering the very gift of salvation itself.

At this particular party, Jesus will offer even more reason for the religious leaders to justify their rejection and ultimate condemnation of Him, while at the same time offering the very gift of salvation itself.

Dinner parties like this had a social order to them. As guests arrived, the host would have arranged customary acts of hospitality for each one. Guests were to be greeted with a kiss, usually on the cheek. They would be provided basins of water and olive oil to wash their feet and possibly a servant from the household to assist them. More olive oil might be provided to apply to one's head and face. Starting with the eldest, guests would then take their places at the table, reclining on long couches or pillows. Guests were to recline on their left side, freeing their right arm to reach for food, with their feet facing away from the table. The guest of honor would traditionally be seated to the immediate right of the host, with the least important guests sitting farthest away from the host and guest of honor.

Only after the traditional courtesies had been extended would the host of the meal offer a blessing of thanks to the Lord. The meal could then be served. Traditional activities would also take place—perhaps music or entertainment and certainly more conversation. At this particular dinner party, the guest of honor would have been expected to further expound on the amazing sermon delivered earlier that day.

## The Unwanted Guest

At this point, someone enters the scene who wouldn't have been a "get" for the dinner party. In fact, this woman wouldn't have made the invite list. She would not have been welcomed to take even the humblest spot at this banquet because she's judged to be unclean, a sinner—at least by Simon and his righteous guests. Somehow she makes it all the way to the feet of the guest of honor. Perhaps others assume she is one of the party servers because she's carrying a flask of oil. But she's there for a different reason, as reflected by the tears that well up in her eyes and run down her cheeks, falling on the feet of Jesus.

Her tears are likely, at least in part, tears of grief for the failures of her sinful life. Simon and others label her a sinner to distinguish her from themselves and thus consider themselves better in the eyes of God and one another, but it's true that this woman had failed to live up to God's Law. We do not know the extent or the nature of her sinfulness, except that it was known throughout the town, but like every other person who has ever lived or will live, she had failed God, failed others, and failed herself. Yet, as her actions will reveal, her tears reflect more than just remorse or guilt over her broken life. They are also tears of humble gratitude, poured out on the One who has addressed her sin.

Her tears reflect more than just remorse or guilt over her broken life. They are also tears of humble gratitude, poured out on the One who has addressed her sin.

Can you imagine this woman's life? Her neighbors reject her, judging her from a safe distance to avoid being labeled unclean by association. She lives as an outcast who regularly receives the disgust of others, with a sense of being worthless in the eyes of God. This woman now comes near to the prophet from Nazareth. Perhaps she overheard people talking about His teaching about God's love for outcasts. Perhaps she heard one of His sermons about God forgiving sinners purely out of His grace for them. As she stands before a room of people who would ridicule her for her sinful life, she stands also at the feet of the One who releases her from her sin. Her tears of sorrow for sin give way to tears of joy for what Jesus has done for her in taking her sins away, in lifting her from the guilt of a broken, unclean life. These are tears of repentance, turning from her sin and trusting in Jesus for forgiveness.

In response to Jesus' amazing love for her, her faith in Him now moves her to action. As her repentant tears wet Jesus' feet, she removes her head wrap in front of everyone—a scandalous act in first-century Israel—and dries Jesus' feet with her exposed hair. She then kisses Jesus' feet and anoints them with the flask of ointment she had brought. Her actions may communicate more than hospitality or even homage. Scripture alludes to kissing as an act of worship (see 1 Kings 19:18; Psalm 2:12). Her anointing of Jesus' feet may have foreshadowed His God-ordained journey to pay the price for her forgiveness. Her actions are humble acts of gratitude toward Jesus, and yet they can communicate so much more about Him. Isaiah writes,

Jesus is good news for this woman, and she anoints His beautiful feet because of it.

"How beautiful upon the mountains are the feet of him who brings good news" (52:7). Jesus is good news for this woman, and she anoints His beautiful feet because of it.

For the host of the dinner, however, her actions—or more accurately, Jesus' lack of action against her for her conduct—communicate all he needs to pass judgment on Jesus:

> **Now when the Pharisee who had invited Him saw this, he said to himself, "If this man were a prophet, He would have known who and what sort of woman this is who is touching Him, for she is a sinner."** (Luke 7:39)

This one verse tells us a lot about the inner workings of Simon and his beliefs. He believes that God would have provided special knowledge to prevent any prophet of His from coming into contact with someone unclean. In Simon's mind, since Jesus did not stop this woman from touching Him or react at all, He obviously did not have insights from God and thus could not be one of God's chosen prophets. If Jesus is no prophet, then the critical Pharisees were correct in their condemnation of Him, and He is not worthy to be the guest of honor at parties like Simon's.

Simon has judged Jesus solely on this encounter with the woman. As Jesus receives this sinful woman in grace, Simon rejects Jesus in self-righteousness. But the party isn't over yet!

## The Prophet's Response

As He frequently does throughout His ministry, Jesus tells a story, this time to address Simon and his faulty judgment.

What's more, His story answers Simon's unspoken condemnation, revealing the special knowledge from God that Simon had been expecting:

> **Jesus answering said to him, "Simon, I have something to say to you. . . . A certain moneylender had two debtors. One owed five hundred denarii, and the other fifty. When they could not pay, he cancelled the debt of both. Now which of them will love him more?" Simon answered, "The one, I suppose, for whom he cancelled the larger debt." And He said to him, "You have judged rightly."** (vv. 40, 41–43)

This parable is simple enough, but it is crucial to understanding the entire dinner encounter. While the one who was released from the greater debt loves more, the moneylender is the agent who acts first! Had the lender not chosen to cancel the debt, that person would not have cause to respond with a deeper love for the moneylender. The moneylender's forgiveness is the act of love that produces a response of love from the one who had been forgiven the greater debt.

This parable is simple enough, but it is key to understanding the entire dinner encounter.

Jesus now applies the lesson to the situation unfolding at the dinner table. He begins with a telling question. "Do you see this woman?" He asks Simon (v. 44). Here, Jesus asks Simon to consider something deeper. When Simon looked at the woman as she washed, kissed, and anointed Jesus' feet, all he could see was her sinfulness, especially when compared to his own supposed righteousness. Jesus saw far more. He saw the woman fully: someone who needed God's unmerited grace, someone who had received His forgiveness of her sins, someone who was responding to His love in her life by showing love to Jesus in her deeds of worship and love, expressed in her hospitality for Him.

This woman opened herself up to even more ridicule by letting down her hair in public and physically touching Jesus, actions that would have been considered inappropriate by the other guests at the table. But she does not show concern for their possible responses. Her focus remains on Jesus, who had acted first in her life with redeeming grace. Like the debtor who owed five hundred denarii, she shows much love to Jesus because He has greatly forgiven her.

By contrast, Simon had shown disrespect to the Lord. Jesus lays it all out plainly:

> **I entered your house; you gave Me no water for My feet, but she has wet My feet with her tears and wiped them with her hair. You gave Me no kiss, but from the time I came in she has not ceased to kiss My feet. You did not anoint My head with oil, but she has anointed My feet with ointment. Therefore I tell you, her sins, which are many, are forgiven—for she loved much. But he who is forgiven little, loves little.** (vv. 44–47)

Despite the hospitality customs of their culture, Simon had extended no acts of love toward Jesus. His actions show he sees no need for Jesus' grace in his life. He had not received Jesus' forgiveness and thus, by implication, remains in his own sin, all the while believing himself to be the only righteous, God-favored one among the three of them.

*Love* is kind of a sloppy word in English, isn't it? I mean, I love my wife. I love my kids. I love my cats. I love theater. I love football. I love cribbage. I love popcorn. I certainly hope I don't love them all the same way! Otherwise someone would feel slighted and others would feel awkward. When I say I love popcorn, I'm not saying that popcorn has gained my faithful devotion. When I say I love football, I'm not saying that my relationship to football touches me to the core of my being (although someone who has watched a game with me might think differently).

I believe that when we say "I love you" to someone, what we mean is "I see you." I see you as you truly are; "I love you" is seeing past the masks we wear so that the world will put up with us, seeing through the lies we tell ourselves so that we can tolerate ourselves. To say "I love you" is to say "I see you as you are in all your failed and frail ways, and I still choose to bless you, even if it comes at the cost of my own blessings." That's love! That's what Jesus extends to the woman at Simon's dinner table. He sees her as she truly is—a sin-fallen person—and He still chooses to bless her with His gift of forgiving, life-saving grace, even though it cost Him His own blessings.

He sees her as she truly is—a sin-fallen person—and He still chooses to bless her with His gift of forgiving, life-saving grace, even though it cost Him His own blessings.

What Jesus says to the woman next at Simon's dinner table expresses that love and sends a shock wave through the other dinner guests.

> **And He said to her, "Your sins are forgiven." Then those who were at table with Him began to say among themselves, "Who is this, who even forgives sins?" And He said to the woman, "Your faith has saved you; go in peace."** (vv. 48–50)

These two short statements to the woman say a lot! In Jesus' parable, the moneylender would easily be seen as God by the dinner guests, since the lender was the one to whom all the debt was owed. As Jesus announces forgiveness to this woman, He places Himself in the role of the moneylender. This implies that everyone who sins—the woman, Simon, and every guest at the table—owes Him a debt. And by announcing forgiveness, Jesus also places Himself in the role of God. Sin, being a violation of God's Law, can only be forgiven by God.

This is why the dinner guests begin to question who Jesus is as the one who forgives sins. For Pharisees like Simon, such claims are tantamount to blasphemy. It is for these very claims that they will seek to bring Jesus to an end, extended on a cross. But Jesus sees this woman. He sees her need for God's forgiving grace, and in love for her as her Savior, Jesus blesses her, knowing that it will cost Him the blessing of life itself. With God's gift of forgiveness of sin, there is salvation, eternal life, and peace with God. The Lord announces these blessings as well and releases the woman to go with God's greatest gifts of love imparted to her!

## Seeing Someone Today

There's a home in Sanford, Florida, where women are truly seen and cared for physically, mentally, and spiritually. Since 2013, Redeeming Life Maternity Home has been welcoming single women who are expecting a child and providing a place to nurture their newborn babies in the love of Jesus. The home was founded by Sheryl and Rev. Ed DeWitt with the help and support of numerous fellow Lutherans. The home is a response in love to the greater gift of forgiving love first given by Jesus to the DeWitts, their family, and those who share in this ministry. The organization has now opened a second home in Dundee, Illinois. At both Redeeming Life Maternity Homes, women and their babies are loved. The staff and supporters of the homes seek to bless these children of our Lord even at the cost of their own blessings, sacrificing their time, talents, and resources so that these women and their children may come to know Jesus' love and forgiveness for them.

I had a chance to tour the home in Sanford. On the tour, the home director drew my attention to a meal chart in the kitchen. Each night, a different mom was scheduled to host a meal for the other moms in the home. The director pointed out to me the significance of these women getting to host and share meals. It builds their confidence in how they will care for their own households one day. It gives them the chance to build a sense of community among the moms as they share a home. It also gives each mom a chance to be *seen*, to realize they are worthy of others preparing a nurturing meal for them because they are loved by their Lord Jesus. Jesus sees these women and their babies. He gives them His gracious love, and in response, they also love much.

Jesus' story and His gifts still find their fulfillment in places like the Redeeming Life Maternity Homes. They also find their fulfillment when we work to truly see the people around us and seek to bring Jesus' gift of grace to them in response to His great love for us. Who in your life might truly be *seen* as someone for whom your Savior died? What an opportunity to warmly welcome them to your table in loving response to Christ's love!

Who in your life might truly be *seen* as someone for whom your Savior died?

Not everybody who merely eats and drinks with Jesus receives the greatest blessings He imparts at the table. Important religious leaders and honored guests dine with the Messiah at Simon's home, but they do so without seeing the need for their own repentance. They do not see their debt owed to the true guest of honor. To them, there is no need for Jesus' forgiveness. They had a meal but not the true fellowship that leads to salvation.

At the same table, a rejected, uninvited guest, a sinful woman, is not welcomed by the self-righteous crowd to sit and dine. Yet her Lord graces her with something that will sustain her to eternal life—His forgiving love. Her repentant heart shows itself in her humble love for Jesus. When we come to Christ's table with a repentant heart, what great things our Lord freely gives! He sees you. He loves you.

## QUESTIONS FOR DESSERT

If you could have a famous guest at your dinner party, who would it be? Why?

How does Jesus communicate that He sees people in your community through the local church you attend?

Whom could you welcome to your table so that they could be truly seen by you and receive Jesus' love through you and your hospitality?

Chapter 9

# THE ROAD TO EMMAUS

*He was known to them in the breaking of the bread.*

— LUKE 24:35 —

**LINDA AND ED HAD EXCITING** news and wanted to share it with friends and family in a fun way. So they planned a backyard barbecue. Linda decorated with color-coordinated streamers, balloons, and tablecloths, Ed set up several backyard games, and they even brought in catered food. As their friends and family enjoyed a wonderful afternoon meal together in Ed and Linda's backyard, a boxed cake was brought out to the main table. Linda requested that everyone find a cup to raise, as she had a toast to make. When the cups were raised, Linda said, "A toast to these simple words: I do!" Ed lifted the lid of the box to reveal a cake decorated with the words "She said yes!"

Shouts of joy and expressions of congratulations began. Linda quickly put on the engagement ring she had tucked away in her pocket and raised her hand high to display it to all. Ed and Linda thoroughly enjoyed sharing their happy news with the people they loved as they hosted this meal. They hoped to host many such meals over a lifetime together as husband and wife.

We often share joyful news over a meal with the loved ones who will rejoice with us. Getting engaged, having a baby, being accepted to a certain school, or landing a new job are wonderful occasions to spend time together in fellowship around food. On a lonely, dusty seven-mile stretch from Jerusalem to Emmaus, two men were on a journey of heartbreak, convinced they had no joyful news to share with anyone. They were joined by a third traveler, who would share that the best news the world has ever known was just beginning to break forth in their presence. And that good news would be revealed to them in the breaking of bread at their own dinner table.

We often share joyful news over a meal with the loved ones who will rejoice with us.

## On the Road

It had been a roller coaster of a week to say the least. The streets of Jerusalem had been packed with crowds from around the Roman world—Jewish pilgrims who had come for the great Passover festival and unwittingly witnessed and likely even participated in events that would change the world forever. They were stirred to line the streets, waving palm branches and tossing their cloaks on the road to honor and welcome the one whom many were saying would rescue Israel: the prophet from Nazareth named Jesus. He entered Jerusalem that day humbly, riding on a donkey and her colt.

He had purposely arranged such an entry, and those who knew the Hebrew Scriptures might have recalled that such imagery was prophesied by Isaiah and Zechariah to describe when the Lord's promised King would come to bring peace to Israel that would even extend to the nations.

As Jesus ascended the Mount of Olives to enter the holy city amidst crowds shouting, "Hosanna to the Son of David!" it seemed that time had arrived. His disciples must have been brimming with anticipation of what glories might await them in the coming days.

How the tables so dramatically seemed to have turned that week! Jesus' disciples had entered Jerusalem that Palm Sunday likely expecting that their rabbi would somehow take His rightful place on King David's throne and begin a reign that would reestablish the kingdom of Israel and return it to its former glory. By the end of the week, they would witness Him experience betrayal by a dear friend, abandonment by His closest followers, a trial by their own religious leaders, and another trial and judgment from the Roman authorities that left Jesus mocked, brutalized, crucified, dead, and laid in a sealed and guarded tomb.

Like anyone who witnesses a traumatic event, these two men cannot escape the gut-wrenching experience.

Now, on the following Sunday afternoon, it looks like everything is over to the two disciples who are making their way home to the town of Emmaus. Like anyone who witnesses a traumatic event, these two men cannot escape the gut-wrenching experience. They talk while they journey, likely replaying the horrific events of the week in their discussion: "How did it end like this? Remember the miracles? His healings and feeding the crowds with next to nothing? People loved Him! They followed Him. *We* followed Him! Why didn't someone come to His defense? Why did our leaders deliver Him to Pilate? Why didn't the Lord stop this?"

As their thoughts and conversation helped them reminisce on their lives with Jesus, the fresh wound of their sorrow and grief would keep drawing them back to the same inescapable reality. Jesus had died. They had heard reports that morning from a few women who had some wild story about His body not being in the tomb and a vision of angels and that Jesus was alive, but these two disciples had witnessed enough. It was over. Their hopes had died with Jesus on Friday, and now there was nothing left but to return home. After all, who holds on to a dead messiah? To move beyond the shocking events of the past week, they would need *outside* help, and of course, the Lord Himself is more than happy to oblige.

It's at this point in their journey when a third traveler joins them. Luke tells us immediately that it is the resurrected Jesus, but the two disciples "were kept from recognizing Him" (Luke 24:16). As Jesus draws near, He initiates the conversation, asking them about their conversation. Although they have already heard the news about Jesus' Easter resurrection, their downcast faces reflect that they have not yet received the news in faith and are still in the deepest pain at their loss.

At this point, Luke introduces one of these disciples to his readers by name: Cleopas. Cleopas responds to Jesus' question with an incredulous question of his own: "Are You the only visitor to Jerusalem who does not know the things that have happened there in these days?" (v. 18). Cleopas's question to

Jesus is rich with irony. He assumes that Jesus is a visitor to Jerusalem, one of the many pilgrims who had come for the Passover. Jesus is indeed a sojourner on the grandest scale! He had come from His Father's right hand in heaven and journeyed for thirty-three years to come to Jerusalem that week. He would soon return to His Father's right hand at His ascension.

However, He had visited Jerusalem not merely to partake in the commemoration of the Passover but to fulfill it by becoming the Lamb of God who rescues from sin and death through His cross. Jesus was the only visitor in Jerusalem who was completely aware of every drop of spit that had hit His face, every voice that had mocked His identity as God's Son, and every sting and pain from the whip, thorns, and nails, which were His cost for the world's salvation. Jesus was intimately acquainted with everything that took place that week! Yet, with a delightful brevity that seems to anticipate the flood of good news about to wash over these two disciples, Jesus simply responds to Cleopas, "What things?" (v. 19).

He had visited Jerusalem not merely to partake in the commemoration of the Passover but to fulfill it by becoming the Lamb of God who rescues from sin and death through His cross.

These men share their understanding of who Jesus was and their misunderstanding of the events of the past week. They knew Jesus to be a prophet whose teachings and deeds were met with favor from God as well as the praise and approval of the people. They knew their religious leaders were the ones who had Him condemned and crucified. But that is where their faith in Jesus seems to fall short. They tell Him, "But we had hoped that He was the one to redeem Israel" (v. 21). To these disciples, Jesus' death is the end of their hopes, despite hearing of His resurrection from the women. They understand their need for redemption from sin and death, but they haven't grasped that it would come by way of God's chosen Messiah being crucified and resurrected.

Even with all these details before them and the resurrected Savior walking alongside them, they still have not grasped the Good News! How will they come to faith? Now, Jesus will use the means our Lord always uses to bring about the miracle of a believing heart: His Holy Word.

> **And He said to them, "O foolish ones, and slow of heart to believe all that the prophets have spoken! Was it not necessary that the Christ should suffer these things and enter into His glory?" And beginning with Moses and all the Prophets, He interpreted to them in all the Scriptures the things concerning Himself.**
> (vv. 25–26)

I've sat at the feet of some great teachers of the Bible, and I've been honored to teach numerous Bible studies, but can you imagine having a two-on-one study of God's Word with the Word made flesh Himself? From this passage, it seems Jesus' focus was on His suffering and resurrection as the Messiah—the very events the disciples were discussing before Jesus joined them. Only now, Jesus will teach these disciples how all the Hebrew Scriptures pointed to and were fulfilled by Him as the Christ who suffered, died, and rose again!

Which passages did Jesus point them to? Did He take them to the sacrifice of Isaac, where the Lord provided a substitutionary sacrifice for Abraham's son? Did He reveal to them the parallel life of Joseph, who through his own suffering was placed in a position to rescue not only his own estranged family but also many nations as they endured a famine? Did He draw them to the prophecy in Micah 5 about an eternal ruler who would come out of Bethlehem? He may have walked them through the powerful account of the death and resurrection of the servant of the Lord in Isaiah 53 or showed them how Hosea 6 revealed God's heart for mercy and even hints at the resurrection on the third day.

Jesus will teach these disciples how all the Hebrew Scriptures pointed to and were fulfilled by Him as the Christ who suffered, died, and rose again!

Personally, I'm looking forward to sitting with these disciples in eternal life and asking them to share the details of that day's journey. Maybe we'll do so over dinner. Whatever Scriptures Jesus highlights, He does so to give these men new understanding. Jesus reveals to them that all the Scriptures speak of Him! He resets their entire orientation toward the Old Testament to understand that it all points to Him, the Messiah, who lived a perfect life, suffered, died on the cross, and rose on third day, fulfilling God's plan of salvation for the world!

Jesus, using the Word of God, brings these disciples from a partial understanding of God's Word to a Christ-centered confession of the Word. He takes them from their lost and misguided messianic hopes to faith in the crucified and risen Lord. As they journey together, He opens the Scriptures to them and brings them from despair to a living hope in their living Lord and thus from death to life everlasting. Thank God Jesus still uses His Word to do the very same for us in our life's journey!

## Mystery Sojourner Revealed

Having received instruction in God's Word to bring them to faith in the Savior who had died for them and now lives to all eternity, these disciples are ready to learn the true identity of their fellow traveler, and it will occur at their table. The details move quickly at this point in Luke's account, but let's slow down to fully digest each portion of the story.

Luke tell us that as the group draws near to Emmaus, Jesus acts as if He is going farther on the journey. What an understatement! Jesus will return to heaven itself in the coming days, but through the Gospel that these disciples will have a hand in sharing, Jesus will journey to the hearts of every believer throughout the world for all time. Jesus is indeed going farther! On the road to Emmaus, realizing Jesus' intent, Cleopas and his companion show some first-century hospitality and urge Him, "Stay with us, for it is toward evening and the day is now far spent" (v. 29).

Jesus graciously accepts their invitation, but He will stay with them in a far greater way than merely accepting their invitation to lodge in their home for the evening.

Jesus graciously accepts their invitation, but He will stay with them in a far greater way than merely accepting their invitation to lodge in their home for the evening. He will abide with His disciples through His Word and Sacraments. There, they will continually encounter the Savior who lived, died, and rose again for them. Even a moment without Him would mean death for His followers, so our Lord promises to stay with them and with us always through these precious gifts of His grace.

The specific wording of Luke 24:29 links the meal the disciples and Jesus are about to eat with two other significant meals in Jesus' ministry: the feeding of the five thousand (Luke 9:12) and the Last Supper (Luke 22:14). In each account, Luke references the ending of the day and sets up a beautiful contrast. Just as the daylight fades away into night, so the light of being alive in this sinful world fades away as the darkness of death comes to each person. Temporary meals like the feeding of the five thousand and the Passover are blessings from the Lord, but they are not enough to give life eternal. Something—or someone—more is needed, and He just entered the house with these disciples. In a few moments, as Jesus takes His place at the head of the table, the light of the world who casts away the darkness of death itself will reveal Himself.

All along the journey to Emmaus, Jesus had been readying His disciples for this moment. Their eyes were kept from recognizing their risen Savior so that He could open their hearts to His Holy Word. Instructed by Christ through His Word about His true identity and mission, they are now prepared to take their place at the table where Jesus gives them yet another gift of His love.

> **When He was at table with them, He took the bread and blessed and broke it and gave it to them. And their eyes were opened, and they recognized Him. And He**

> **vanished from their sight. They said to each other, "Did not our hearts burn within us while He talked to us on the road, while He opened to us the Scriptures?"** (vv. 30–32)

In taking the bread and offering the blessing, Jesus becomes the host, taking on the role that would normally be done by the head of the house. The language Luke uses to describe Jesus' actions here mirrors the language of the Last Supper, when Jesus instituted Holy Communion. And while this meal at Emmaus was not a celebration of Communion, the connection is abundantly clear. Jesus is recognized in the *breaking of the bread.* He will be recognized, present, in His gift of Holy Communion, where the blessings of His life, death, and resurrection are brought to His disciples throughout time. A simple meal, to be sure, but the promise and presence of Jesus is there. As Jesus is recognized in the breaking of the bread in the Lord's Supper, His disciples receive Him in the eating of His body and drinking of His blood, and we receive all the promises He attaches to this meal: forgiveness, life, and salvation. The Emmaus meal is a beautiful reminder of the greater meal of the Sacrament.

## Seeing with Opened Eyes

As we linger at this dinner table, Luke gives us yet another gem: "Their eyes were opened." This expression relates back to earlier in the story, when the disciples' eyes were kept from recognizing Jesus on the road. But it also draws us back to the meal that first brought sin and death to the world. When

Adam's and Eve's teeth first sank into the flesh of the fruit from the tree of the knowledge of good and evil, Moses records, "Then the eyes of both were opened, and they knew that they were naked" (Genesis 3:7). The fall of humanity into sin and death now has the Lord's full response in His resurrected Son! The eyes of His followers are now opened not to sin but to the gift of salvation that God has given in Jesus and His means of grace, the Word of God and Baptism and Communion. May our eyes always be opened to recognize our Savior in these gifts He's given us!

The fall of humanity into sin and death now has the Lord's full response in His resurrected Son!

I find it wonderful that these two disciples don't seem to marvel at the miraculous way Jesus leaves their presence. What consumes their thoughts is how Jesus opened the Scriptures to them and how their hearts burned within them as He did so. While He did disappear from their sight, He would remain with them through the Word He had taught them.

The joy they had just experienced moved them to share it with Jesus' other followers. Luke tells us that, even though the day was nearly spent, these disciples leave their home that hour to return to Jerusalem to meet with the apostles and those gathered with them. They then learn the good news that the risen Savior has also appeared to Simon Peter, confirming for them their own resurrection encounter. And what do they note as significant for the other disciples? Jesus' teaching on the road and how He was known in the breaking of the bread, a model of how the church throughout time will know the Savior.

The Emmaus story—with God's Word moving the disciples on the road from disbelief to faith in the suffering and glorified Savior and with a Christ-centered meal at the center—paints a beautiful picture of our own journeys. Where are you in your journey home? Are you struggling to believe Jesus' death and resurrection are the hope of your redemption? Are you at a point where the journey seems long and lonely? Does the light of life's journey seem nearly spent, leaving you longing for home and the nourishing meal that awaits?

The Emmaus story—with God's Word moving the disciples on the road from disbelief to faith in the suffering and glorified Savior and with a Christ-centered meal at the center—paints a beautiful picture of our own journeys.

Jesus knows we need Him to impart to us the gift of faith, so He draws near to us along life's journey through His Word and Sacraments. In them, He teaches us that He is the fulfillment of God's plan for our redemption. May our hearts burn with the Word He teaches us, and may that Word open our lips to speak His Good News to others. May our eyes be opened to recognize Him in His Holy Supper, which sustains us with His forgiving grace throughout our life's journey until we finally arrive at His eternal home.

Then our Lord will hospitably welcome us to His table. At that meal, He will not vanish before our eyes. He'll pull up a chair right next to you and put food on your plate, and the celebration will have no end! Till then, your Savior stays with you on life's road, and the Table in His house is always filled with a life-sustaining Meal for you.

## QUESTIONS FOR DESSERT

How do people today have a misguided or incomplete picture of Jesus? What despairing conclusions can come from these misunderstandings?

What are some of your favorite stories or passages of Scripture that bring home for you the reality of who Jesus is?

How does Jesus draw near to join people on their journey of life today?

Chapter 10

# BRINGING THE LOST TO THE TABLE

*This man receives sinners and eats with them.*

— LUKE 15:2 —

**IN FEBRUARY 2004, *THE PASSION OF THE CHRIST*** hit theaters. Some moviegoers were touched to see such an artistic, if graphic, portrayal of the last few days of Jesus' life. Others were upset and offended, believing the film had antisemitic themes that once again cast Jewish people as those responsible for Jesus' death. I was serving as pastor in Mount Prospect, Illinois. We saw an opportunity to witness the Gospel.

My senior pastor at the time, Rev. Marc Schwichtenberg, developed our plan. One evening a week, we would go to the coffee shop a few blocks from church. We let the community know that we'd be there to discuss the movie. We also informed the members of the congregation that we'd be happy to discuss the movie with them at church, but if they wanted to be part of the coffeehouse evenings, we expected them to invite an unchurched family member or friend to join them at our table.

Once a week during the movie's run, Pastor Marc and I would grab a drink and a pastry and take our place at a booth or table. It wasn't a full dinner, but it was always a full house. As we talked with the people who snagged seats at our table, the rest of the shop would fill up. The other patrons would remain at their tables until we were done, listening in on our conversation, and we always stayed until the shop closed. We prayed that our Lord would use those evenings to deepen the faith of believers and draw others closer to the truth of Christ's death and resurrection for salvation. But here's what struck me: as Jesus moves His followers to faithfully, winsomely, and publicly speak of Him, who else might He draw near to *overhear* the witness of His Gospel?

As Jesus moves His followers to faithfully, winsomely, and publicly speak of Him, who else might He draw near to *overhear* the witness of His Gospel?

Those tense, truth-telling evenings at the coffeehouse remind me of an event in Jesus' own incarnate mission.

## Teaching at Tables

Time and again in his Gospel account, the evangelist Luke draws our attention to Jesus' practice of welcoming people to dine with Him. As might be expected, His disciples regularly ate meals with their rabbi, but Jesus welcomed a much greater circle to His table. Luke reveals that the downtrodden and the outcast were often guests where Jesus dined. Some who were graciously welcomed to Jesus' table were labeled by the Pharisees as "tax collectors and sinners" (Luke 15:1), which set up a continuing tension between Jesus and this self-proclaimed righteous group of religious leaders. We see this tension in Luke 15, but the details are set up for us in chapter 14.

There, Jesus is teaching the crowds what it means to follow Him and the cost of being His disciple. He concludes His teaching with these words: "He who has ears to hear, let him hear" (Luke 14:35). At the start of Luke 15, we see the people who were coming to hear Jesus: "Now the tax collectors and sinners were all drawing near to hear Him. And the Pharisees and the scribes grumbled, saying, 'This man receives sinners and eats with them'" (vv. 1–2). Regularly in Jesus' ministry, He would combine the practice of hospitality through meals with the opportunity to teach His guests while reclining at the table. And just as regularly, we catch images of Pharisees and scribes leveling this complaint. From their perspective, Jesus welcoming and eating with sinners was more than just a social faux pas. Jesus' willingness to show such hospitality to those who were known as sinners could have contributed to the Pharisees' understanding of why He would deserve death.

Regularly in Jesus' ministry, He would combine the practice of hospitality through meals with the opportunity to teach His guests while reclining at the table.

Luke 15 captures that imagery of Jesus dining with sinners and Pharisees listening in but refusing to join. As these groups who see themselves quite differently hear what Jesus says in the parables of this chapter, let's take our place around Jesus' proverbial table to listen to His teaching.

## Bringing Home a Sheep

As Jesus begins to tell the parables in Luke 15, He is aware that He is addressing two audiences: those who are labeled as sinners and those who would do the labeling while seeing themselves as righteous. The first parable poignantly addresses both groups.

In this parable, a shepherd has a hundred sheep but has lost one of them. Jesus frames the parable by asking His two sets of listeners to consider what they would do in that situation. Would they leave the ninety-nine in the open country and go after the lost sheep until it was found? His audiences could easily picture the sacrifice this would pose: wandering around in the hot, rugged Judean countryside, seeking out the one lost sheep. Sheep are not the brightest of animals, so this seeking is vital for the life of the sheep; if the shepherd doesn't find the sheep first, a predator eventually will. Once the sheep is found, the shepherd carries it home, rejoicing, and calls his friends and neighbors together to rejoice with him.

At this point, someone else seems to have taken on the role of the shepherd. Rather than the people gathered to listen, Jesus Himself is the Good Shepherd. He finds us lost in our sin, places us on Himself, and carries us all the way to salvation, rejoicing along the way! As He does so, He invites everyone to rejoice in the salvation we've received from Him. Jesus tells His listeners the heavenly application, just to make sure they get the point: "Just so, I tell you, there will be more joy in heaven over one sinner who repents than over ninety-nine righteous persons who need no repentance" (Luke 15:7).

What is going on before the Father's throne in heaven? There is more joy over the one who repents than over the far greater crowd of people who consider themselves righteous and thus see no need to repent. Jesus' audiences must now consider two things: how does the sheep repent in the parable, and what exactly does it mean to repent? The lost sheep does nothing in and of itself to repent. All the work is done by the shepherd. The shepherd seeks, the shepherd finds the lost and carries them home, and the shepherd invites the community to rejoice.

The shepherd seeks, the shepherd finds the lost and carries them home, and the shepherd invites the community to rejoice.

It's a beautiful image of our Lord's work among us, His lost sheep. He does not expect us to contribute one thing to our own salvation. He does all the work for us as our Good Shepherd, using His Word to turn our hearts away from our sin to trust His blood-bought gift of redemption. Jesus always does all the work in bringing His lost ones home. There's more joy over the work He's done in even one lost person's life to bring him or her home than over ninety-nine people who refuse to believe they're lost and in need of repentance, thinking they are righteous in God's eyes. They've absented the role of the Good Shepherd from their lives. But the feast is in the home of the Good Shepherd, and it's the lost He brings there, so if the "righteous" need no repentance, then they don't need Jesus. They won't be in His home, and there is nothing to feast and rejoice over.

## Finding a Lost Coin

Jesus intensifies His point with a second parable. He asks His audiences to consider the actions of a woman who had ten coins but lost one of them. Jesus rightly proclaims that any woman in that situation would light a lamp, bust out a broom, sweep the floors, and make a careful search of the entire house until she found the lost coin. Imagine losing something valuable to you, like your wedding ring or a family heirloom. You'd likely move at least a piece of furniture or two in your search. I know we did when it happened to my wife!

Upon finding the lost coin, the woman's actions are similar to the shepherd's in the first parable. She calls her friends and neighbors together to celebrate with her that what was lost is found. We didn't throw a party for the neighborhood when we found my wife's wedding ring (though maybe we should have!), but there was certainly much rejoicing in our house.

Again, just in case His listeners haven't grasped the theological application, Jesus tells them the point: "Just so, I tell you, there is joy before the angels of God over one sinner who repents" (v. 10).

The structure of the second parable is much like the first: the characters lose something of theirs, search for what was lost, and invite their community to share in their joy when they find it again. Both parables illustrate the eternal joy in heaven over the matter of repentance, of turning from sin and trusting in the Lord's rescue from it. Like the sheep, the coin does nothing in and of itself to repent of being lost. Could you imagine the coin frantically waving its little arms and calling out in a tiny voice, "No, I'm not over there! Sweep over here!

Bring your lamp over here so it can catch the glint of my shininess!" Of course not! The work of finding the coin is done completely by the woman.

But who is the woman in this parable? If Jesus can readily be seen as the shepherd in the first parable, perhaps this woman represents His church.[4] Moving forward in time, our Lord will not only seek the lost to bring them home but also bring His followers into that joyful task. Like the woman with her lamp, the church shines the light of the Gospel as we proclaim and teach the truth of God's Word. As we read in Psalm 119:105, "Your word is a lamp to my feet and a light to my path." Jesus calls us to diligently search for the lost that, by the work of the Spirit, they, too, might turn from sin and trust in the Savior, who has done everything that they should be found for eternal life. And like Jesus, we joyfully invite the community around us to come into God's house and rejoice with us and with angels and archangels and all the company of heaven as the lost are found by our Lord!

Like Jesus, we joyfully invite the community around us to come into God's house and rejoice with us and with angels and archangels and all the company of heaven as the lost are found by our Lord!

## A Father and His Lost Son

Jesus' third parable brings elements from the first two parables to a climax that illustrates His mission of forgiving

4 For more on this idea, see Just Jr., *Luke 9:51–24:53*, 591.

grace for salvation. The stakes are higher this time—not just animals or money, but a man's own children.

Jesus tells them of a father who has two sons. The younger son asks for his share of the inheritance. In other words, the son says to his father, "Why aren't you dead yet so I can get what's coming to me?" Jesus' first listeners would likely have judged such a disrespectful son as deserving death. Yet Jesus says the father does something shocking. He consents to his son's request and divides his property between his sons. The younger son then gathers all he has and sets off for a faraway country, where he blows the inheritance in reckless living.

There's a lot to unpack here. In a time when most wealth was based on having land and what it produced, the younger son would likely have had to sell off his part of the family farm in order to take his assets abroad. This might seem insulting and shocking to us, that he'd wish his father dead and sell off part of the family farm, but in Jesus' day, it would be downright scandalous. Setting off for a faraway land also meant he wound up among the unbelievers, the Gentiles, where he took the blessings of his father and the gifts of God and squandered them foolishly. The "sinners" gathered to hear Jesus' teaching would likely have identified with such foolish choices.

The "sinners" gathered to hear Jesus' teaching would likely have identified with such foolish choices.

But then, Jesus continues, the young man's money runs out and a famine hits. The man's situation radically changes from well-resourced party-thrower to a stranger in need. Trying to address his situation himself, the younger son hires himself out to feed pigs. It gets so bad that he longs to eat the pods that the pigs were eating, but no one gave him anything.

What Jesus describes here is a worst-case scenario for His first audiences. They would have seen working with pigs as unclean because pigs were unclean animals, not to be dealt with by God's righteous people. And to eat what the impure pigs were eating (which wouldn't even have been nourishing for the man in the first place) would have been disgusting to all. Nor was the man guaranteed any wages for his unclean, pig-feeding work. A day laborer might have their wages withheld for any number of reasons, and as a foreigner, this man would have had no recourse if that happened. The younger son's situation could not be bleaker. He needs to be rescued. He needs his father's grace.

What Jesus describes here is a worst-case scenario for His first audiences.

Now Jesus gives a pivotal point in the younger son's story:

> **But when he came to himself, he said, "How many of my father's hired servants have more than enough bread, but I perish here with hunger! I will arise and go to my father, and I will say to him, 'Father, I have sinned against heaven and before you. I am no longer worthy to be called your son. Treat me as one of your hired servants.'"** (vv. 17–19)

Note here how our Lord is behind every aspect of this young man's eventual return home. Had the Lord not sent a severe famine, the son might never have considered returning to his father's house. Sometimes our Lord puts us in a place of trial to get our attention. Like a lost sheep or coin being found, even this son's return is all God's doing. The man resolves to go back to his father, and he formulates what he believes will be a worthy repentance. But his rehearsed repentance hints at the idea that he might somehow earn his way back into his father's house—something like "Give me a chance, and all the grief I've caused, I'll work it off." It leaves the possibility that, as he becomes like a hired servant in his father's house, he will not be relying on his father's grace.

But now Jesus paints an amazing picture of steadfast, faithful love as He turns the focus of His audiences to the father in the story. While the son was "still a long way off, his father saw him and felt compassion, and ran and embraced him and kissed him" (v. 20). We can imagine the father standing day after day, looking out on the horizon, hoping to catch a glimpse of his son's return, and then coming to him with an embrace and kiss that communicates forgiveness. Notice, too, how the father's acts of mercy and forgiveness all happen before the son gets to blurt out one word of repentance. The father humbles himself by running to his "sinner" son, robes flying, as he meets his son and confers on him acts of love that show everyone his son has been welcomed back home. Just like the lost sheep and coin, the lost son is brought home solely by the actions of the one who was searching for him: his father. All three parables present an image suggestive of Jesus Himself, who comes right to where His people are, the place of sin and death, to bring us

Just like the lost sheep and coin, the lost son is brought home solely by the actions of the one who was searching for him, his father.

His rescue of forgiveness, even at the cost of His own dignity as He willingly hangs exposed, naked on a cross.

Surrounded by the father's forgiving grace, the tenor of the son's confession changes: "Father, I have sinned against heaven and before you. I am no longer worthy to be called your son" (v. 21). He cannot earn his way back into his father's house because it was never about the squandered inheritance. It was about the lost relationship, which can never be regained by good works, no matter how earnestly they are offered and done. But there is no need for that. In forgiveness, the father has already fully restored his son. It cost the father personally and dearly, but his grace is freely given in joy as he welcomes his son back home and restores his place in the family.

The father has his son dressed to reflect his restoration. Shoes are put on his feet (for slaves did not have shoes; sons did), and a ring is put on his hand (signifying his authority as a member of the household). And the son is clothed in the best robe—an image that reminds us today of our Baptism, where Jesus' robe of righteousness is placed over us and we are restored to His family.

Now the time has come to celebrate. The fattened calf is sacrificed, a life given up in thanks to God for the son's life, which has been restored. Let the feasting begin!

## A Father and His Other Lost Son

Not everyone wants to join the feast though. (Sound familiar?)

Jesus turns the focus of the parable once more, this time to the older son. Coming in from the fields, the older son hears the party in full swing. When he learns the reason for it, he gets angry and refuses to enter the house and take part in the celebrations over his brother's return. To our modern ears, this may seem like an understandable point in the plot. There's always sibling rivalry. The older son is portrayed as faithfully staying home and not squandering the family inheritance. Perhaps some jealousy or a feeling of favoritism may come into play in the older son's response.

Jesus' first audience may have heard the story differently. To them, the older son was likely disrespecting his father. If the father of a household held a party, it was the oldest son's obligation not only to attend the party but also to be the head steward of the banquet. He was to honor his father by ensuring the food was prepared, the guests were comfortable, and the drink was plentiful, allowing his father to focus on celebrating with the guests.

While the father could have punished his older son, he again humbles himself by going out to speak to him. Their dialogue illustrates that the older son, too, has lost his relationship with his father. He says he's slaved for his father all these years. He sees himself as righteous because he never disobeyed his father's commands and portrays his father as self-indulgent and unjust. He complains to his father, "You never gave me a young goat, that I might celebrate with my friends. But when this son of yours came, who has devoured your property with prostitutes, you killed the fattened calf for him!" (vv. 29–30). The older son clearly has a bad opinion of his brother, painting him with much harsher terms than Jesus used earlier in the parable. I suspect the Pharisees and scribes spoke in the same outlandish ways about the guests gathered at any dinner where Jesus welcomed "tax collectors and sinners."

The father could rightly rebuke his son. But the father is patient and loving, even while offering a corrective word to his self-righteous child. He reminds his son of his actual place—that all that the father has is the son's as well. Yet he also reminds his son of the greater value, which is found in a relationship with the father and his family, and the joy that comes with restoring a lost member of that family: "It was fitting to celebrate and be glad, for this your brother was dead, and is alive; he was lost, and is found" (v. 32).

He also reminds his son of the greater value, which is found in a relationship with the father and his family, and the joy that comes with restoring a lost member of that family.

Throughout Luke, Jesus is seen feasting with those whom He has welcomed to the table by His grace, even as another group gets angry and refuses to come to the table—much like the sons in this parable. We don't know where this parable was told. But imagine if this parable had been told by our Savior on a given night when He had invited all to dine with Him, around a table filled with people who were considered sinners yet whom He had joyfully welcomed. And just outside, others grumbled and refused to come in because of those already seated at the table. If that was the case, then the example of these two sons and the meaning of this parable would have been stunningly clear to those listening that night!

## Still Bringing the Lost to the Table

Did you notice how Jesus leaves the third parable unresolved? Does the older son come in or not? Perhaps Jesus left it unresolved because He knew He would continually encounter people throughout His incarnate ministry who were graciously welcomed but refused to come to His table. Perhaps Jesus left it unresolved because this is a tension that will exist for His church until His return. Our Lord's Gospel invitation goes out to all, and by the work of His Spirit through His Word and Holy Baptism, some enter His house, rejoicing to hear Him speak of His love for them even as He feeds them His Holy Meal at His Table. And Jesus rejoices in heaven each time you and I come into His house and receive His grace.

Yet our Lord always has His eyes on the horizon, looking for children of His who haven't come home. They may be out there because of actions that would merit the label "sinner." They may be out there because they see themselves as righteous and in no need of repentance. They may be out there because they don't like the others in the house. They may be out there simply because they're lost and have no idea the party is for them as well. Our Lord longs to seek out each of them and bring them to His feast.

Our Lord longs to seek out each of them and bring them to His feast.

In love, He equips and invites us, His church, to seek along with Him so that His dinner table might be full. And in grateful response, we light our lamp and start sweeping. Let us always rejoice when a lost one is brought home. And may our brothers and sisters in Christ also rejoice when you and I are the lost ones brought home!

## QUESTIONS FOR DESSERT

Where do you get to talk about Jesus in a public setting? How might your conversations be used by God to impact those who overhear them?

______________________________________________

______________________________________________

______________________________________________

______________________________________________

______________________________________________

How do Jesus' parables in Luke 15 ready us to deal with scandalous sinners? the openly self-righteous?

______________________________________________

______________________________________________

______________________________________________

______________________________________________

______________________________________________

How might your church more intentionally reflect Jesus' joyful welcome to His people as they are brought home? What could you do to get that going?

______________________________________________

______________________________________________

______________________________________________

______________________________________________

______________________________________________

Chapter 11

# THE LAST SUPPER

*I have earnestly desired to eat this Passover with you before I suffer.*

— LUKE 22:15 —

**I LOVED JANET DEARLY. SHE WAS** a close family friend and like a big sister to me. The summer after eighth grade, I ended up "on loan" to Janet as a live-in babysitter and general house helper. Her husband was away serving in the Army, and Janet was often called in to work at night. My own adopted parents had been foster parents, and it seemed like there was always a baby or toddler in our home, so by age 14, I was well-versed in caring for little ones. Janet felt confident I could help her. I would spend nights at their place so that she would have the freedom to go to work while I stayed with the baby.

Janet was not a Christian at the time, yet she and her husband still had a large, illustrated Bible in their home. Sometimes when Janet would come home from work at night, she'd pop open the Bible, point to a picture, and ask me to tell her about it. Fresh from six years of Lutheran elementary education, including two years of catechetical instruction, I was happy to tell the biblical stories on which my faith was founded. I didn't realize it was a witnessing relationship, but the Lord was using it to draw Janet to His Gospel.

That same year, I was confirmed at Christ Lutheran Church in Peoria, Illinois. Like many Lutheran churches, the custom at Christ was for young people to receive Holy Communion for the first time following their confirmation, and so it was for me. A short while after my confirmation, I was again spending the night at Janet's. My only recollection of what happened that evening came from Janet the next morning.

Janet had come home late and found me asleep on their living room couch. As she gently tried to wake me so I could move to the guest bedroom, apparently I looked her in the eyes and said, "I received it from Him."

Janet, unsure what I was talking about, asked me, "What did you receive?"

The fact that I was talking about receiving the body of Christ in Holy Communion even while half asleep left a deep impression.

Still sleepwalking, I responded, "The body of Christ," and shuffled into the guest bedroom.

The fact that I was talking about receiving the body of Christ in Holy Communion even while half asleep left a deep impression on Janet. She wanted to talk more about what the Sacrament meant to me, and it led to yet another opportunity for Jesus to draw her a little closer to Himself.

But that morning talk with Janet about what I had received the previous Sunday in worship was sparked long before that day. It was launched in a large upper room some two thousand years before with a meal that would change the world!

## A Large Upper Room, Furnished

The details of the meal that took place in that large upper room are too rich and wonderful to cover every precious point in one chapter. That said, allow me to share a few impressions of what unfolds as we watch from the doorway of this familiar room.

As the Scriptures lead us into the upper room, we find an intimate setting. Gone are the crowds seeking the amazing power of Jesus in miraculous displays. Gone are the religious leaders of the day challenging Jesus and stewing in silenced, murderous anger at His responses. Here, Jesus gathers His closest followers to celebrate the Lord's rescue. They had gathered for the Passover, the meal they partook of each year that brought into their lives the Lord's rescue of His people from Egypt through the death of the firstborn son and the saving blood of the lamb. Jesus' disciples likely thought this would be another chapter in that line of annual celebrations.

The Passover was to be celebrated with one's family, and that is what these followers are. They are Jesus' family, even as He had previously taught them: "Whoever does the will of My Father in heaven is My brother and sister and mother" (Matthew 12:49). Jesus had expressed to His disciples that He earnestly desired to eat this Passover meal with them before He was to suffer, and He will fulfill the role of the head of the household for this meal. What is about to unfold is personal for everyone in human history and for Jesus Himself. Jesus,

God Incarnate, is about to die. He indicates time and again throughout this meal that He is fully aware of what is about to take place. Jesus had fulfilled all righteousness, having obeyed God's Law without sin. He would now fulfill His Father's gracious plan for the world's salvation by being the Lamb of God whose sacrifice would cleanse us from sin. And as God tied His deliverance of the past to the meal this spiritual family had gathered to celebrate, so Jesus would tie His act of salvation to a meal like no one had ever known.

As God tied His deliverance of the past to the meal this spiritual family had gathered to celebrate, so Jesus would tie His act of salvation to a meal like no one had ever known.

Details in the four Gospel accounts give us some sense of the room's layout. The Scriptures record that the Last Supper took place in a large upper room that had been furnished and was ready. Such furnishings may have included short-legged tables and low-lying couches or pillows on which to recline. We read in John 13:21–26 that Jesus' beloved disciple John reclined at His side that evening, and Peter was likely nearby as well. Judas, too, was close by—close enough to receive bread dipped in the same dish as Jesus.

However they were arranged, whom does Jesus gather together for one final meal before His Passion? They're His closest followers, yet they are sinners, and through them, expressions of sorrow, self-delusion, arrogance, denial, and betrayal will find their place around Christ at His table.

As Jesus looks around this table where He will offer the greatest meal ever given in the world, whom does He see? He sees His apostles. They are the ones who will deliver the Good News of Jesus' death and resurrection to the world. In just a few days, Jesus will send them into the world even as the Father sent Him (see John 20:21–23). But on this night, the apostles will abandon Jesus, and one of the Twelve will be the instrument of His betrayal.

On this night, the apostles will abandon Jesus, and one of the Twelve will be the instrument of His betrayal.

None of this comes as a surprise to Jesus. He is the one who tells them about their falling away and about His betrayer among them. Eleven of the twelve men are filled with sorrow at the thought of any of them betraying Jesus. "Is it I, Lord?" they each ask. The way they word the question indicates that they expect Jesus to say no, and it seems they're ready to supply their own answer. "Lord, I am ready to go with You both to prison and to death," Peter says (Luke 22:33), and Mark shares in his Gospel that everyone around the table says the same thing. In their blustering denial, even Jesus' closest followers reflect ignorance about what will soon happen and arrogance about their own strength and loyalty to the one who has brought them to the meal.

## Teaching Humility

Jesus sees Peter. Over the past three years, for better and for worse, Peter has asserted himself as leader among the Twelve. In that leadership role, Peter has uttered some amazing things by the revelation of God. "You are the Christ, the Son of the living God," he confessed (Matthew 16:16). When Jesus asked the Twelve if they wished to leave Him along with the crowds, Peter responded, "Lord, to whom shall we go? You have the words of eternal life, and we have believed, and have come to know, that You are the Holy One of God" (John 6:68–69).

However, it seems that Peter considered himself almost on equal footing with Jesus or at least as a self-appointed protector of Jesus—the disciple who could tell Jesus what to do. In one of their first encounters, Peter told Jesus to go away from him because he realized he was a sinner (see Luke 5:1–11). It was a strange mix of humility and arrogance; Peter realized he was sinful and Jesus is righteous, yet he was telling Jesus what to do. When Jesus told His disciples that He was going to Jerusalem to be betrayed, killed, and rise to life, Peter took Jesus aside and began to rebuke Him: "Far be it from You, Lord! This shall never happen to You" (Matthew 16:22). Right after the focus of this chapter, when they're in the Garden of Gethsemane, it's Peter who, seeking to "protect" Jesus, will draw his sword and clumsily strike the high priest's servant, Malchus, cutting off his right ear (which Jesus immediately heals to prevent the scuffle from becoming an all-out blood bath in which His disciples would have been executed on sight). Here in the upper room, Peter will be true to character and again mix pride and love, humility and arrogance as he interacts with his Lord.

In the course of the meal, Jesus does a surprising thing. He rises from supper, lays aside His outer garments, ties a towel around His waist, pours water into a basin, and begins to wash the disciples' feet. Jesus will teach the significance of this action as He speaks with Peter, but before we get there,

In the course of the meal, Jesus does a surprising thing.

let that image sink in. At the Last Supper, the meal where He institutes the giving of Himself to His followers for all time, Jesus offers Himself as a humble servant, stripped of clothing, in order to wash His followers clean. We see this image again hours later as He hangs on the cross, humiliatingly stripped of His clothes, taking the role of the Suffering Servant. Both actions—later on Good Friday and here at the Last Supper—are completely of Jesus' own choosing. As Jesus had said earlier, "I lay down My life that I may take it up again. No one takes it from Me, but I lay it down of My own accord. I have the authority to lay it down, and I have the authority to take it up again" (John 10:17–18).

Jesus offers Himself as a humble servant, stripped of clothing, in order to wash His followers clean.

As Jesus comes to Peter to wash his feet, Peter objects. In what is likely a mix of love and pride, Peter cannot fathom having Jesus stoop to such a lowly act of service. He tries to take charge of Jesus' actions and prevent Him from washing his feet. Peter even bluntly tells Jesus, "You shall never wash my feet." Jesus patiently leads Peter to a deeper understanding of His actions, telling him, "If I do not wash you, you have no share with Me" (13:8). Like all sinners who will be saved, Peter must receive the cleansing gift of Jesus' mercy, which comes through His humiliation as our Suffering Servant. In his zeal, then, for what Jesus seeks to do, Peter again attempts to control Jesus' work. Peter responds, "Lord, not my feet only but also my hands and my head!" (v. 9). And Jesus again corrects him.

Peter is learning that he is not in charge of how our Lord gives His grace. Thankfully, Jesus is! He acts without the prompting or directive of even His closest followers, and His cleansing for sinners is complete. Yet, even as Jesus washes His disciples' feet, He declares that not all of them are clean. There is a betrayer among them.

## Betrayal Among Friends

Peter and Judas have a strangely close connection. Earlier in His ministry, Jesus had linked each of them to the one who lurks in the shadows of the Last Supper—Satan. When Peter had sought to prevent Jesus from going to Jerusalem to die for salvation, Jesus rebuked him: "Get behind Me, Satan!" (Mark 8:33). Another time, when Jesus had questioned His disciples about whether they would continue to follow Him, Jesus said, "Did I not choose you, the twelve? And yet one of you is a devil." John makes it clear that Jesus was referring to Judas (John 6:70–72). Jesus calls one apostle Satan and the other a devil.

Satan had been pursuing both men for his own evil purposes. At the Last Supper, Jesus declares that Satan had demanded of God to have Peter (Luke 22:31–32), and John tells us that when Jesus gave Judas the morsel of dipped bread, Satan entered Judas (John 13:27). Luke makes it clear that Satan had also entered Judas earlier, when Judas first conspired with the religious leaders of the day to turn Jesus over to them (Luke 22:3). Jesus intercedes for Peter's life. Even to Judas, it seems Jesus gives a last word of warning: "The Son of Man goes as it is written of Him, but woe to that man by whom the Son of Man is betrayed! It would have been better for that man if he had not been born" (Matthew 26:24). After Peter denies even knowing Jesus three times during His trial, Peter turns back in repentance. But Judas, seeing Jesus condemned to death, takes his own life.

We do not know what moved Judas to go from one of Jesus' closest followers to the one who would betray Him. Perhaps it was greed. John reveals in his Gospel account that Judas had been in charge of the disciples' moneybag and used to help himself to it (12:6). But thirty pieces of even the highest-valued silver of the day would be, at best, only a few months' salary for a laborer. Perhaps Judas believed it was an easy profit; even if he colluded with the religious leaders, Jesus could slip free as He had done in other threatening situations. Or perhaps Satan entered Judas and duped him into believing the accusations of the religious leaders—that Jesus was in league with the devil and had been casting out demons by the power of Satan. If that were the case, Jesus would be a false prophet and thus deserve death! Regardless of the motivations, Judas eventually realizes what he's done. "I have sinned by betraying innocent blood," he tells the chief priests when he attempts to return the bribe (Matthew 27:4).

Whatever motivated Judas, imagine the heartbreak our Savior must have felt when an apostle He had chosen in love rejected His gifts, resulting in that apostle's death. John captures the sorrowful moment between Savior and betrayer so well: "After receiving the morsel of bread, [Judas] immediately went out. And it was night" (John 13:30). The darkest hour had come. Satan had gained power

Imagine the heartbreak our Savior must have felt when an apostle He had chosen in love rejected His gifts, resulting in that apostle's death.

over one of the Messiah's closest followers in an effort to kill Him. Yet, in that dark moment, all was unfolding according to God's plan of salvation in fulfillment of His Word.

## Prepared for Mission

Some eight hundred years before that night, the prophet Isaiah wrote, "The people who walked in darkness have seen a great light" (9:2). At the dinner table in that large upper room, Jesus clearly sees Himself surrounded by the darkness of His followers' sin. They are prideful, arrogant, short-sighted sinners who will all flee in fear, leaving Jesus alone to carry out the work of salvation. Yet the focus at the table is not on them but on Jesus Himself, on the words and actions that He will use to equip and supply His followers, both those at that table and those who will come after them.

John makes it abundantly clear that Jesus knows all things. Jesus knows what is happening to Him that week. He knows He is soon to return to the Father. He knows that His disciples will be God's chosen vessels to bring the Gospel to the world. He'll even tell them on Easter (just three days away) that He is sending them in the same way that the Father had sent Him into the world (see John 20:21). Knowing all this, Jesus takes a great deal of time at this meal to ready His followers for their mission after His earthly ministry. Jesus covers more ground in John 13–17 than we can address here, but let's digest a few choice morsels of His teaching.

Jesus takes a great deal of time at this meal to ready His followers for their mission after His earthly ministry.

In washing their feet, Jesus tells them that this act of humble service is an example of how they are to care for one another. Does that mean that Christians should wash one another's feet? Yes, if that's the care our fellow believers need! But Jesus makes a deeper point in His teaching. With this service, He orders the disciples' place in life. He tells them that a servant is not above his master; in other words, if Jesus, their Lord, has so humbly served them, they are not to think too highly of themselves but rather to serve one another humbly with Christlike care. Jesus also states that a messenger is not above the one who sent him. Jesus' followers will not only be servants. They will also be messengers. He will send them out with the greatest message of all: God's gift of redemption through Jesus! And His messengers will not go out alone with that Good News. God Himself will be with them. Jesus tells them, "Truly, truly, I say to you, whoever receives the one I send receives Me, and whoever receives Me receives the one who sent Me" (John 13:20).

But if Jesus is not among them visibly, how will people know they are His messengers? At the table that night, Jesus gives His disciples a new commandment that they are to love one another. The Lord had commanded His people to love one another in the Old Testament, but Jesus goes deeper: "Just as I have loved you, you also are to love one another. By this all people will know that you are My disciples, if you have love for one another" (vv. 34–35). As the dinner guests around Jesus' table go on to demonstrate a humble, servant-oriented, self-sacrificing, graciously-forgiving-on-account-of-Christ love

> The world will identify Jesus' followers when they love like Jesus.

for one another, they show themselves to be Jesus' disciples. The world will identify Jesus' followers when they love like Jesus.

Are their Christlike works done to somehow complete Jesus' work for their own salvation? Not at all, as the Lord reveals in John 14. Jesus is going to prepare a place for them in His Father's house. He will return and take them there. They will come to that place of eternal life completely by Jesus' work, as He tells them: "I am the way, and the truth, and the life. No one comes to the Father except through Me" (v. 6). Their Christlike love for one another on display for a world that doesn't know Jesus will come as the result of Jesus being *in* them. Jesus teaches them that night that they will do even greater works than He has done in His earthly ministry. But how can that be? It will be true because Jesus is going to the right hand of the Father. There Jesus will glorify His Father by doing whatever His disciples ask in His name. Their being Christlike comes from Jesus' continuing work on their behalf and through them.

## United to Christ

How will this be possible? The people around Jesus' table that night—and everyone who will follow Him through them—are still sinful people who sin every day. What's more, they will be going into a world that is lost in sin and will hate them for being followers of Jesus. How will this group do greater things than Christ in being His messengers to the world? He will not leave them to such a mission by themselves. In fact, He will not be separated from them by the slightest degree.

Jesus will unite Himself so closely with His followers that we will actually become part of His body (see 1 Corinthians 12:12–27). This is revealed powerfully in what Jesus teaches at the Last Supper and in what He gives at His table. Jesus first teaches about this inseparable bond by promising His disciples a Helper, the Spirit of truth, whom Jesus will ask the Father to send to His disciples. The Holy Spirit will continuously equip Jesus' disciples with His Word. Jesus tells them the Spirit will bear witness to Him as the Savior, both for their own faith and as the content of the message they'll share with the world. Jesus assures those gathered at His table, "You know Him, for He dwells with you and will be in you" (John 14:17).

In the very next verse, Jesus tenderly promises that He will not leave His followers to be orphans but that He will come to them. The image is rich with loving hope. A child becomes an orphan when his or her parents die, and indeed, Jesus knows that by the following afternoon, He will be hanging dead on a cross. Like children losing their parents, His disciples will be struck with profound grief on Good Friday. However, Jesus gives them another promise of His resurrection. He will not leave them in an orphaned state but will rise from death and come to them that they, like Him, might live beyond death itself. Until that time of eternal life, Jesus, in love for us, promises that He and His Father will make their home with us. "If anyone loves Me, he will keep My word, and My Father will love him, and We will come to him and make Our home with him" (John 14:23). It's a beautiful

Until that time of eternal life, Jesus, in love for us, promises that He and His Father will make their home with us.

image to think of our bodies as the place where the Father and Son make their home, living in us. The Father and Son make their home wherever we are so that we are never alone as God's children.

Jesus gives yet another illustration of this intimate bond between His followers and Himself. In John 15, He states that He is the vine and His followers are the branches. A vine is the source of life for its branches and the source of nourishment for the fruit each branch produces. Without our bond to Jesus, we can neither be alive nor bear any fruit. And so Jesus teaches at His table that night, "Whoever abides in Me and I in him, he it is that bears much fruit, for apart from Me you can do nothing" (v. 5).

Finally, Jesus' high priestly prayer in John 17 emphasizes the intimate relationship between Jesus, the Father, and Jesus' followers. Jesus concludes their time in the upper room with this prayer. In it, He declares that the hour has come and asks His Father to glorify Him so that He might in turn glorify His Father. This mutual glorification will happen because Jesus will do what is needed to give eternal life to all who are His by dying on the cross, rising to life, and returning to the presence of His Father. Because Jesus will return to the Father, He tasks His followers with sharing the message of salvation with the world around them. Again, Jesus will not leave them by themselves in this joyful yet daunting task. He asks His Father for a connection with His followers that defies the imagination:

> **I do not ask for these only, but also for those who will believe in Me through their word, that they may all be**

> **one, just as You, Father, are in Me, and I in You, that they also may be in Us, so that the world may believe that You have sent Me. . . . I in them and You in Me, that they may become perfectly one, so that the world may know that You sent Me and loved them even as You loved Me.** (vv. 20–21, 23)

These are signs that Jesus is fully connected to His followers and they to Him: having the Holy Spirit dwelling in their hearts, with His continual work of bringing their thoughts back to all that Jesus had taught, and seeing the fruit of faith in them as their thoughts and actions take on more and more of a Christlike way, especially as they tell the message of His Gospel and forgive one another.

Yet our Lord has another amazing gift that will unite His people to Himself in a real, incarnate way for all time in all places and for each member of His Body, the church.

## A Meal Like No Other

That night in the upper room, Jesus' disciples had gathered to celebrate a meal of deliverance that connected them to the past acts of the Lord's salvation as He rescued His people from Egypt. Jesus had brought them there to give them a gift that would fulfill that past, tie His church to the events of Holy Week, and remain with them into the future until His glorious return. Centuries before, the prophet Jeremiah wrote of the gift Jesus was giving at the Last Supper:

> **Behold, the days are coming, declares the LORD, when I will make a new covenant with the house of Israel and the house of Judah, not like the covenant that I made with their fathers on the day when I took them by the hand to bring them out of the land of Egypt, My covenant that they broke, though I was their husband, declares the LORD. For this is the covenant that I will make with the house of Israel after those days, declares the LORD: I will put My law [Torah] within them, and I will write it on their hearts. And I will be their God, and they shall be My people. And no longer shall each one teach his neighbor and each his brother, saying, "Know the LORD," for they shall all know Me, from the least of them to the greatest, declares the LORD. For I will forgive their iniquity, and I will remember their sin no more.** (31:31–34)

The Lord had established an old covenant with His people through the prophet Moses. He had given His Law, written on stone, and established a system of blood sacrifice not only to ratify the covenant but also to forgive their sins. His people had broken that covenant again and again; they were never able to fulfill the Law. Yet the Lord remains faithful and promises a new covenant that He Himself will fulfill through His own sacrifice. The blessed result, as Jeremiah prophesies, is that the Lord will write His Torah—His

Yet the Lord remains faithful and promises a new covenant that He Himself will fulfill through His own sacrifice.

Word—on His people's hearts so that they will truly know Him and He will forgive them!

Now at His table in the upper room, Jesus, the Word made flesh, will put His very body and blood into His followers' mouths as He gives the gift of Himself. Jesus declares that the cup of wine that night is His own "blood of the covenant, which is poured out for many for the forgiveness of sins" (Matthew 26:28). Paul, decades later, summarizes what Jesus gave His church that night:

> **The Lord Jesus on the night when He was betrayed took bread, and when He had given thanks, He broke it, and said, "This is My body, which is for you. Do this in remembrance of Me." In the same way also He took the cup, after supper, saying, "This cup is the *new covenant* in My blood. Do this as often as you drink it, in remembrance of Me."** (1 Corinthians 11:23–25, emphasis added)

At Jesus' word, the bread He gives them is His body, which will be given on the cross and rise from the dead for their salvation. At Jesus' word, the wine He gives them is His blood, which is shed on the cross for their forgiveness and courses through His resurrected body. Nothing now can separate Him from them. No sin, no guilt, no broken covenant, nothing, because Christ has done all for their redemption. The Word in, with, and under the bread and wine enters the very mouths of His followers through the Supper He institutes. They chew upon His body and drink His blood so that the one who forgives them and gives them life might be with them right down to the very cells of their bodies, so that Jesus might be with them always, to the end of the age.

At the Last Supper, Jesus fulfills His promise of the new covenant. He has taught His followers His Word. He has washed them in His forgiveness and set an example of humble service. He has fulfilled His promise to be with them both for their own salvation and for their mission of bringing His life-saving message to others in the abiding presence of His body and blood, which they will again and again receive inside themselves as they come to His Table.

At the Last Supper, Jesus fulfills His promise of the new covenant.

In fact, as they come to His Table to receive Him for their own forgiveness, Jesus' followers will be giving their public witness of His death, resurrection, and coming return. Paul proclaims, "As often as you eat this bread and drink the cup, you proclaim the Lord's death until He comes" (v. 26). What Jesus begins at His table in the upper room in the meal of Himself goes with His church from that day forward, an uninterrupted gift from generation to generation. We come to this same Table to receive in our bodies this same amazing meal of Christ and His gift of forgiveness, life, and salvation! Like the Lord feeding His people in the wilderness for forty years with the manna from heaven, our Lord promises to feed us of Himself, a foretaste of the feast to come, and He will do so until He returns to fulfill this Holy Meal's gift to its fullest completion!

My friend Janet did not have a long earthly life. She died in her early forties from an undiagnosed heart issue. But before she died, by the work of the Holy Spirit through His Word, she had come to know Jesus as her Savior and often had dined on

His body and blood for her forgiveness, life, and salvation. I was honored to have played some small role in our Lord bringing her to the feast He began in the upper room. I trust that Janet, now gathered to her Lord, joyfully awaits the day when we will all dine together at His feast that will have no end. Until that day comes, may we joyfully confess to the Janets in our lives, "I've received it from Him, the body of Christ," and watch as our Lord bears fruit from our confession.

## QUESTIONS FOR DESSERT

How is the Last Supper a picture of the church as we celebrate the Lord's Supper?

How does knowing that Jesus is always with you strengthen you to be His witness?

What does it mean to you that you receive Jesus' body and blood?

CHAPTER 12

# FULLY NOURISHED: OUR MEALS TODAY

*Wisdom has . . . set her table. . . .*
*She says, "Come, eat of my bread*
*and drink of the wine I have mixed.*
*Leave your simple ways, and live,*
*and walk in the way of insight."*

— PROVERBS 9:1, 2, 4–6 —

**MAYBE IT REALLY DID START** with attached garages and central air, where people could pull right inside their garage, walk into their climate-controlled home, and never even have to say hi to their neighbors. Maybe it's our lack of real community as people more and more turn to virtual connections to form relationships with others. Maybe it's our busyness and the convenience of fast food.

It's clear that people are gathering less often to share a meal with others. And when people do sit down for a meal with others, there are fewer and fewer people around the table.

But I don't think we were designed to be this way on a regular basis.

Take a moment to ponder creation from the perspective of God Almighty. We've come full circle, back to where we began in chapter 1 in the Garden of Eden. Our Lord had all eternity to consider the creation He would bring forth from nothing, and whatever He would create, it would be perfect by His design. In all the universe, He created a planet and placed it at just the right spot in a solar system He created and endowed it with all the elements and characteristics necessary to sustain life. He then filled that planet with an abundance of plants and animals, all created according to His will. Then He created the amazing creatures that would bear His image, humans.

In God's perfect, sinless world, He created humans in such a way that they would take in nourishment by eating: "And God said, 'Behold, I have given you every plant yielding seed that is on the face of all the earth, and every tree with seed in its fruit. You shall have them for food'" (Genesis 1:29). God could have designed humans to acquire nourishment and sustain life in a variety of ways. He could have designed us to be sustained only through His continuing direct power as the giver of life, without any nourishment from other parts of His creation. He could have designed us to filter nutrients through the air as we breathe or receive the same

In God's perfect, sinless world, He created humans in such a way that they would take in nourishment by eating.

life-sustaining elements as we drink water. He's God Almighty! He could have created humans to have some special organ in our feet that would sift what we needed to sustain life directly from the soil as we walk! Yet our Lord did not design us in any of those ways when it came to receiving nourishment to sustain life.

Why did God create us this way?

One answer might include the idea that our Lord set limits on His perfect, image-bearing creatures to continually remind them of two important things. First, they were not equals of their Creator. While He had endowed humanity with a nature that reflected His own, they were not the creators. They were to live (indeed, had to live) within the limits He had established for all created life. Second, they would be able to see time and time again as they lived within God's established limits that He is a generous, gracious, life-giving God. His creatures needed Him to give them all they needed to support this body and life, and our Lord would demonstrate His faithful provision each day. The planet, fresh water, proper oxygen levels, even the processes within our very bodies necessary to sustain life—all would continue to function by the gift of our Creator God.

All would continue to function by the gift of our Creator God.

Therefore, God's image-bearing creatures would not only depend on Him but even grow through the daily experience of life itself to know that He is a dependable, trustworthy God. That would further mold His creatures' response to be like Him in how we'd serve and bless the rest of His creation. We would love because He first loved us. Martin Luther puts it so well in his explanation of the First Article of the Apostles' Creed: "All this He does only out of fatherly, divine goodness and mercy, without any merit or worthiness in me. For all this it is my duty to thank and praise, serve and obey Him. This is most certainly true."

Yet all of this could have been revealed and accomplished without giving us the gift of eating. By creating us to eat food, our Lord blessed us with something deeper. Air, water, even biological systems all sustain life. But eating does something more than merely sustain biological life. Eating invites the opportunity to build relationships with others, relationships that can become a community where we each find welcome. As people sit down for a meal, they are able to share their life experiences with one another. They have a place to tell their stories, share their insights, or simply enjoy the blessing of being with others at the table. We can certainly sustain our physical lives through the task of eating, but when we share a meal, we are nourished in so many other ways.

When we share a meal, we are nourished in so many other ways.

Food affords us the chance to be gracious, loving, and even compassionate as we invite others to partake of what we've helped provide for them. While our Lord certainly provides all the elements on earth that produce its bounty, He also allows humanity to play a role in producing that daily bread through our various vocations. What a blessing it is to reflect His grace and love by bringing others to our table! Welcoming others to our table is more than feeding them what has been provided by our Lord through us. We also experience together the dignity of being invited to the table, not because any of us have earned such a place but simply because we are loved by our Lord and by those He has placed in our lives to share life around His life-sustaining gifts. When we are invited to a meal, our Lord gives us the chance to humbly receive from others. When we are the host of a meal, we have the opportunity to reflect our Lord's grace in giving to those at our table. As we share food and stories around the table, we can speak of our Lord, who has given it all to us—the means, the meal, those gathered at the table, and life itself.

Our world and even the church today are mired in many problems. Reexamining our view of meals could be a building block to start addressing some of those problems. Think of the difference if, even a few times a week, we allowed our meals to be places where we're fully nourished. It could be a chance to hear the invitation of our Lord to come and be filled, feasting together on His gracious gifts of food, fellowship, and the opportunity to share His Word. It's a chance to invite others to come and be filled by those same gifts from Christ! God's Word encourages us to practice hospitality (see Romans 12:13; Hebrews 13:2), which almost always includes sharing a meal. Allow me to encourage you with a few ideas as you consider how your meals might provide deeper, Christ-centered nourishment.

## Fully Nourished with Solo Meals

When eating alone, you're never alone.

You can't gather with guests, tell stories, and share the fuller life at every meal. However, when the pace of life and its circumstances have you eating by yourself, enjoy the guest of honor, who is always with you. Take a moment to acknowledge that Jesus is right there in you! If you're baptized into His name, you are clothed with Christ. You are a temple of the Holy Spirit, who renews that covenant of Baptism in your life each day. If you're a partaker of Holy Communion, you have physically, sacramentally received Jesus' body and blood into your own body. It doesn't get much more connected than that! Jesus Himself promises, "If anyone loves Me, he will keep My word, and My Father will love him, and We will come to him and make Our home with him" (John 14:23). The triune God has made His home with you.

As you sit down for your "solo" meal, be still for a moment and let the mystery of knowing that you are dwelling in your Savior God, and He in you, become part of your mealtime. Now that you've acknowledged the Lord is right there with you, it's a great time to talk with Him. Thank Him for the meal, of course, but why not let your meal with Jesus unfold like it might if you were having a meal with a close friend or family member?

Let the mystery of knowing that you are dwelling in your Savior God, and He in you, become part of your mealtime.

Speak to Him about what's going on in your day. Share what's on your heart. Bring up joys and concerns you have about loved ones. Talk to Him about conflicts you're having. Ask Him to be with you in those moments and remind you that He is there. If you're eating in public, talk to Jesus about the people you notice there. Ask Him to mold how you interact with them. If you want to hear Jesus speaking back to you, take a few moments during your meal and read a portion of Scripture.

Now it's not a meal on your own or one merely filled with emails and social media on your phone. It's a meal you've been able to have with your Savior, the Savior of the world. That kind of meal brings fuller nourishment than merely eating food.

## Fully Nourished as a Family

Intentionally set times each week for family meals.

It may sound like an obvious thing, but in our world today, putting something on the schedule means it's more likely to happen. Ask the rest of your family to make it a priority to be at those meals as well. You may not be able to eat with your family every day. If your family is used to eating two or three meals a week together, see if you can make that three or four and so on. When possible, try not to let your mealtimes be hurried events as you're pressed to get to the next thing. It may help to schedule both a start and a stop time. Knowing there will be an ending time to an activity (including meals) allows some minds the freedom not to worry about how long the current activity is taking.

While at the table, encourage the thought of sharing your greater life as a family by telling stories and inviting others to do the same. You might ask family members to share a story about something that made them laugh that day or something that touched their hearts. Ask everyone around the table to share what goals they have for the week or what they're hoping for in the near future.

As your questions and stories help others around the table open up to share more of life together, remember Jesus is also at your table. Jesus dwells in you and every other believer at the table! Jesus also promises, "For where two or three are gathered in My name, there am I among them" (Matthew 18:20). As you call on Him in thanks for the meal, Jesus is at your table. Include Him in your life as you eat. Ask your family where they saw Jesus in their lives that day. Talk about where you each see a need for Jesus' grace and love in someone else's life. It might be that someone needs to hear and receive Jesus' forgiveness through you. It might be that you need to risk the vulnerable place of seeking Jesus' forgiveness through someone else. Gathering for a meal might be an ideal time to have meaningful discussions as you support your loved ones with Christlike love.

Jesus dwells in you and every other believer at the table!

Ask any children at the table what they'd like you all to pray for and remind them of Jesus' presence at that meal. Remind them that Jesus is there because He loves each of you, and by His grace, He's made you part of His family. How does knowing that Jesus is with you temper how you deal with one another? As always, if you want to hear Jesus speak to you at your meal, read a portion of His Scripture and discuss what Jesus is saying in that passage.

When we spend time with Jesus at each meal, He helps us grow deeper in our connection

When we spend time with Jesus at each meal, He helps us grow deeper in our connection to Him and our connection to one another as His family.

to Him and our connection to one another as His family. Over time, our meals then take on a much richer depth and satisfaction as we walk in the insights of wisdom Jesus sets before us (see Proverbs 9:6).

## Fully Nourished with Meal Guests

Who else would Jesus welcome to your table?

You've probably got an acquaintance or casual friend who doesn't know you're a follower of Jesus. But that relationship could grow over burgers and potato salad! A neighbor who struggles with loneliness or a lack of friends would be tremendously blessed by an invitation from you to come to your table. This may not be a daily or even weekly occurrence. But what if we reimagine our dinner tables as places where Jesus extends His care and love for others through us? How might knowing that Jesus is going to be there enrich both our guests' and our experiences of sharing meals as a community? How might our Savior serve a generous helping of His love and grace through such gatherings?

What if we reimagine our dinner tables as places where Jesus extends His care and love for others through us?

Consider consistently setting aside a day or two each month to invite a few friends who might not know Jesus to share in the daily bread our Lord has provided for us. As your friends learn that they're always welcome at your table, how might this lead to a hospitable welcome to Jesus' home? Just having those experiences with friends at our tables is a wonderful blessing. How much deeper and more joyful when we see that our relationship with Jesus is part of that gracious welcome and part of our lives together at the table!

We can pass the coleslaw to friends and neighbors and talk about His grace for us all, realizing with joy that such meals are a foreshadowing and a picture of the promised eternal future in Christ.

## Feasting Forever

I have a luncheon appointment for two million years from now with Dave.

Dave was an amazing man whom I had the honor of getting to know in my early days as a pastor. He put his faith in Christ into action in his work as a top executive of a large company. He had designed and built his own home (which was jaw-droppingly beautiful), and his hobby was restoring old sports cars. Dave had a gift for hospitality and regularly and joyfully welcomed me to his home. In my time serving as Dave's pastor, he developed brain cancer. I watched, prayed, and brought Dave Christ's Word and Sacrament as the disease robbed him of his energy and strength, his gifts, and the ability to even do the simplest of tasks as his memory began to fail him.

One day, I was at Dave's home to share with him Christ's grace, and the reading that came up was Mark 2:1–12, the account of Jesus healing the man who could not walk. I thought it might be a tricky text to share with Dave as he was close to death and physical healing might not be in his near future. However, our Lord is gracious and drew my focus to the reality that, in that healing account, Jesus first forgives the man. He then provides physical healing.

"That same rhythm," I told Dave, "is found in your life."

Jesus had given Dave forgiveness, from his Baptism to every encounter with Christ's words of absolution to even the Meal of His body and blood that I had brought him. Because of Jesus' forgiveness, healing would come for Dave. It may not have come through doctors and nurses, but it would come at Christ's return when, like the man who could not walk, we'd hear something very similar from our Lord: "Get up and go home."

At that point in our visit, I had a suggestion. "Dave, I want you to plan on having lunch with me in two million years."

He looked at me as if he thought his young pastor had been out in the hot sun for too long.

> "I want you to plan on having lunch with me in two million years."

"Think about it," I said. "Because of Jesus' forgiveness for us both, in two million years, you'll have been with our Lord in eternity for about two million years, and I also will have been with our Lord for about two million years. I don't think after that amount of time our Lord will mind if you and I have lunch together. Let's plan on it!"

For the first time during that visit, Dave smiled. He turned to his wife, Anne, and said, "Honey, will you write that in my day planner? I'll probably forget."

Do you know who will not forget? Our Savior, Jesus! Whether it is two million years until His return or ten million or just a few years from now, I imagine Jesus, on some glorious day in eternity, will remind Dave and me of our plans for lunch.

In fact, I'm sure Jesus will join us for the meal, and the time around the table that afternoon with the three of us will be fully nourishing.

Start filling your eternal day planner by bringing someone to your table today, where Jesus will join you for a meal and nourish you both.

## QUESTIONS FOR DESSERT

What are some creative ways you could practice the Christian value of hospitality?

Whom would you love to see at your table on a regular basis? for eternity?

# ACKNOWLEDGMENTS

I am grateful to my Lord Jesus that He would call me in the waters of Holy Baptism to be His own and then further bless me with the opportunity and ability to write anything that would glorify Him. I pray this book will do just that for every reader.

I am also deeply grateful for the amazing team with which He has surrounded me. They have contributed their time, their skills, and their patience in helping bring about this project. I wish to thank Marguerita, my wife, for her encouragement to write in the first place and her patience as the days stretched to weeks and months to complete this book. Thanks to Rev. Dr. Jeff Leininger and Rev. Brian Davies, who both encouraged me to bring this book to Concordia Publishing House for consideration. Thank you to my amazing editor, Jamie Moldenhauer, who diligently read my rough draft and brought her skills to bear to make the polished book you now hold. Thank you also to the entire team at CPH who helped to take the vision of this book and make it a reality. Finally, thank you to my dear sisters and brothers in Christ of the Lutheran Women's Missionary League who first requested that I write a Bible study on this book's topic many years ago.

To God be the glory!

# BIBLIOGRAPHY


Aland, Kurt, Matthew Black, Carlo M. Martini, Bruce M. Metzger, and Allan Wikgren, eds. *The Greek New Testament: Third Edition (Corrected).* United Bible Societies, 1983.

Albrecht, G. I., and M. J. Albrecht. *People's Bible Commentary: Matthew.* Concordia Publishing House, 1996.

Bailey, Kenneth E. *Jesus Through Middle Eastern Eyes: Cultural Studies in the Gospel.* InterVarsity Press, 2008.

Bailey, Kenneth E. *Poet and Peasant.* Eerdmans, 1976.

Bailey, Kenneth E. *Through Peasant Eyes.* Eerdmans, 1980.

Baumler, Gary P. *The People's Bible Commentary: John.* Concordia Publishing House, 2010.

Engelbrecht, Edward A., ed. *The Lutheran Study Bible.* Concordia Publishing House, 2009.

Gibbs, Jeffrey A. *Matthew 1:1–11:1.* Concordia Commentary. Concordia Publishing House, 2006.

Gibbs, Jeffrey A. *Matthew 21:1–28:20.* Concordia Commentary. Concordia Publishing House, 2006.

Just, Arthur A., Jr. *Luke 1:1–9:50.* Concordia Commentary. Concordia Publishing House, 1996.

Just, Arthur A., Jr. *Luke 9:51–24:53.* Concordia Commentary. Concordia Publishing House, 1997.

Luther, Martin. *Luther's Small Catechism with Explanation*. Concordia Publishing House, 1986, 2017.

Maier, Paul L. *In the Fullness of Time*. Kregel Publications, 1991.

Maier, Paul L., ed. *Josephus: The Essential Works*. Kregel Publications, 1988.

Matthews, Victor H. *Manners and Customs of the Bible*. Hendrickson Publishers, Inc., 1988.

Michaels, J. Ramsey. *The New International Commentary on the New Testament: The Gospel of John*. Eerdmans, 2010.

Stevenson, Struan. *The Course of History*. Arcade Publishing. 2017, 2019.

Wright, N. T., and Michael F. Bird. *The New Testament in Its World*. Zondervan Academic, 2019.

Voelz, James W. *Mark 1:1–8:26*. Concordia Commentary. Concordia Publishing House, 2013.